JOSHUA, MOSES AND THE LAND

JOSHUA, MOSES AND THE LAND

TETRATEUCH-PENTATEUCH-HEXATEUCH
IN A GENERATION SINCE 1938

by

A. GRAEME AULD

T. & T. CLARK
36 GEORGE STREET, EDINBURGH

Printed in Scotland by
Clark Constable (1982) Ltd., Edinburgh
for
T. & T. CLARK LTD., EDINBURGH

ISBN 0 567 09306 9

First printed 1980, Reprinted 1983

PREFACE

No canonical arrangement of the Bible links the book of Joshua with the five 'books of Moses', although traditional Christian ordering of the contents of the Bible may have been less explicit than Jewish usage in separating the Pentateuch from the following books about the past.

Yet it has been commonplace in modern criticism to treat study of Joshua as an appendix to—when not an integral part of—study of the Pentateuch. And this has been the case at least since Stähelin detected[1] de Wette's 'Elohist'[2] in the book of Joshua too. Wellhausen shows support for this trend in the very title of his classic study, *Die Composition des Hexateuchs*, even if his cautious observation has often been overlooked that Joshua, while an appendix to the Pentateuch assuming the latter at all points (and so distinct from the books Judges to Kings), does *not* consist of the same material edited in the same way.[3] Any thorough account of the history of scholarship in this matter would require an independent volume —this one limits itself to the discussion since 1938.

The first three chapters document an *impasse*. The first traces the development of Noth's contribution to understanding Joshua and the Pentateuch. The second analyzes Mowinckel's restatement of a Hexateuch hypothesis. The third surveys the attitudes to the literary relations of Joshua and Numbers found in introductions, commentaries, and special studies; and it takes particular interest in the literary implications of a series of studies of the geographical material in the second half of Joshua.

Such concentration on Noth and Mowinckel needs no defence. Noth broke some quite new ground; and his works have served as point of departure and continued point of reference for such subsequent study. Then Mowinckel's is the most comprehensive rebuttal of Noth's attempt to deal with Joshua as distinct from most strata in the Pentateuch; his renewed plea that Joshua be recognized as culmination of a 'Hexateuch' is often quoted with at least limited approval, despite serious flaws in the presentation of his argument. Our third chapter provides some of the documentation for Kaiser's claim that students of Joshua are faced with a choice between Noth and Mowinckel till the appearance of a new analysis.

This *impasse* appears to be due more to the inherent difficulties of the relevant texts than to mistaken application of Pentateuchal theories. The next three chapters offer a new detailed discussion of these texts. They represent and illustrate a much more positive attitude than has been current in recent scholarship to the Septuagint version of Joshua, which is taken to reflect in the main an earlier edition of that book than our inherited Hebrew text—and, if so, a better platform than the latter for viewing the shape and development of the book. Those familiar with Wüst's studies of the biblical texts relating to the geography of the settlement will recognize the stimulus they have provided to the fourth and fifth chapters. These come to very different conclusions, but are deeply indebted to his resolute wrestling with Noth's inheritance. The sixth chapter raises explicitly the question whether Pentateuchal strata appear in Joshua, and discusses the final stages of the production of the Pentateuch itself.

The concluding seventh chapter reviews the main conclusions of the study, and considers some of its wider implications. In particular it seeks to relate these conclusions to some of the latest contributions to Pentateuchal criticism. These studies could have been reviewed in chapter three, but it seemed more convenient to describe their arguments against the background of some of our own.

The contents of this volume are quite varied. It moves from a review of scholarship to a detailed discussion of the drafting of some Hebrew texts to a consideration of some wider implications. It is the case—and deliberately so—that the argument hangs on some of the central textual conclusions. And proper assessment of these is possible only for the Hebraist. Yet the work has been presented in such a way that the wider argument can be read on its own: the more technical discussion appears in smaller type in the middle chapters, in such a way that the main text makes sense without it (provided that the reader takes the details on trust!).

It is intended as a preliminary piece of Pentateuchal criticism that affirms Noth's methodical progress to the Pentateuch from Joshua via the final chapters of Numbers, although not all his arguments and conclusions. Even where specific proposals are not offered it is supposed that other parts of Pentateuchal tradition were developed in ways similar to those detailed here. Many readers with literary, religious, and historical interests will detect (or suspect) a wealth of corollaries to the book's main results. A few have been mentioned or at least hinted at. To develop adequately its possible implications for our understanding of Israel's tribal system, or canonical developments, or the role of the remembered past within early Israel and Judaism would have required a vast tome. But perhaps more important, these very familiar concerns might have diverted attention from my main proposal: that our approach to all these topics may be clarified by renewed attention to a series of broadly parallel texts and largely similar developments in Numbers, Joshua, and elsewhere.

This study is dedicated to the memory of Père Roland de Vaux who supervized the first stages in its research and took a friendly interest in its development. To two others a considerable debt is also gratefully acknowledged. Professor Rudolf Smend's Münster seminars taught me how to read the book of Joshua. And Professor George W. Anderson, one of my first Old Testament teachers, the supervisor of my doctoral thesis—in several respects but a progress report of this study—and my present head of department, has encouraged the project from beginning to end.

Thanks are due also to those but for whom the following would have remained a private typescript. In particular I record the enthusiasm and support of Messrs. T. & T. Clark; then the printing advice of Mr. Alec Muir of Messrs. Morrison & Gibb; and finally the grant towards publication of my own university.

University of Edinburgh
Summer 1980

NOTES

1. Stähelin, 'Beiträge', pp. 461ff.
2. de Wette, *Beiträge.*
3. Wellhausen, *Composition*[3], p. 116.

CONTENTS

ABBREVIATIONS

ASTI	Annual of the Swedish Theological Institute (Jerusalem), Leiden.
ATD	Das Alte Testament Deutsch, Göttingen.
BHS	Biblia Hebraica Stuttgartensia.
BWANT	Beiträge zur Wissenschaft vom Alten und Neuen Testament, Stuttgart.
BZAW	Beihefte zur Zeitschrift für die Alttestamentliche Wissenschaft, (Giessen) Berlin.
ExT	Expository Times, Edinburgh.
FRLANT	Forschungen zur Religion und Literatur des Alten und Neuen Testaments, Göttingen.
HAT	Handbuch zum Alten Testament, Tübingen.
IEJ	Israel Exploration Journal, Jerusalem.
JBL	Journal of Biblical Literature, Philadelphia.
KS	Kleine Scriften.
LXX	Septuagint.
MT	Massoretic Text.
OTL	(SCM) Old Testament Library, London.
OTS	Oudtestamentische Studiën, Leiden.
RB	Revue Biblique, Paris.
SOTS	Society for Old Testament Study.
StTh	Studia Theologica, Oslo.
ThLZ	Theologische Literaturzeitung, Leipzig.
ThR	Theologische Rundschau, Tübingen.
ThZ	Theologische Zeitschrift, Basel.
VuF	Verkündigung und Forschung, München.
VT	Vetus Testamentum, Leiden.
VTSuppl.	Supplements to Vetus Testamentum, Leiden.
ZAW	Zeitschrift für die Alttestamentliche Wissenschaft, Berlin.
ZDPV	Zeitschrift des Deutschen Palästina-Vereins, Leipzig, Wiesbaden.

CHAPTER I

VON RAD AND NOTH

A. Von Rad: The Hexateuch

The modern phase of the discussion of the relationship between the book of Joshua and the Pentateuch was ushered in by two brilliant studies published in 1938. The first of these was Gerhard von Rad's essay 'The Form-critical Problem of the Hexateuch',[1] written in the hope that fresh attention to the form of the Hexateuch as a whole might point the way out of the stalemate he detected in Hexateuchal studies. Von Rad's exposition is lengthy but his basic argument is both straightforward and very familiar; and so it need not detain us long.

He starts with the observation that the final form of the Hexateuch, despite the intricate elaboration of this tremendous edifice, is quite simply a 'history of redemption' or a creed. Indeed one can readily believe that its origins belong to a type of literature of which we have several examples in the OT: the short historical creed. Deut. 26:5b–9 is the classic example of these—a creed still linked to its situation in worship. Deuteronomy preserves another in 6:20–24; while Joshua's farewell speech uses yet a third (Jos. 24:2b–13). The considerably greater detail of this third example demonstrates the flexibility of the basic form; and examples from the Psalter, like Pss. 136 and 105, show both that still greater detail is possible within a relatively short compass and that elaboration of the form took place within the orbit of the cult.

Even the shortest form of the creed in Deut. 26:5–9 mentions patriarchal beginnings, the oppression in Egypt, the deliverance by Yahweh and his bringing Israel into the promised land. What is immediately striking when this summary of the faith is compared with the Hexateuch is that all the main constituents of the latter are present in it except for the Sinai revelation—and this remains true of all OT examples of this genre until the great prayer of Neh. 9:6ff., where 'at last we find a passage of the kind which hitherto we have everywhere sought in vain'.

The implication that the Sinai material has roots different from the history of salvation appears to confirm Wellhausen's finding: 'Clearly visible behind the work of the Yahwist is a form of the tradition in which the Israelites moved on to Kadesh immediately after the crossing of the Red Sea, without first making the expedition to Sinai.'[2] And von Rad adds that even were Wellhausen's hypothesis not demonstrable on purely literary grounds, this would not affect our recognition that the Sinai tradition is essentially an independent entity within the Hexateuchal tradition. The openings of both the Blessing of Moses (Deut. 33) and the Song of Deborah (Jud. 5) offer confirmation of this in their testimony that the constitutive element of the Sinai tradition is the coming of God, not the wanderings of the people. This observation points in its turn in the direction of von Rad's next deduction: that the Sinai narrative is the cult-legend of a particular festival—in fact (following Mowinckel's work on the Decalogue)[3] the New Year Festival. Indeed, when the agglomeration of different strata is set aside, and the basic form of Deuteronomy is studied, it becomes apparent that it shares the same underlying shape as the older Sinai narrative in Exodus—so providing independent testimony to the form of the festival liturgy from which both derive. Links between Jos. 24 and Deut. 27 persuade von Rad that the Sinai narrative had its origin in the Feast of Booths as celebrated at Shechem.

The settlement tradition—that other pillar of the Hexateuch—von Rad locates in the Feast of Weeks as celebrated at Gilgal: in part because of the explicit mention of first-fruits in Deut. 26, and in part because of the Benjaminite and even Gilgalite locus of most of the traditions of settlement in Jos. 2–11.

These traditions of settlement and Sinai had only been capable of developing so far in their original cultic milieu. Their co-ordination as part of a monumental literary enterprise—one which involved too the addition of much originally heterogeneous material—freed these traditions for the quite new development evidenced in the successive literary strata of the Hexateuch. Von Rad gives the Yahwist the credit for this breakthrough. He it was who both inserted the Sinai tradition into the settlement tradition and prefaced this new whole with a primeval history—so achieving the lineaments of the structure familiar to us.

Von Rad is in no doubt but that this remarkable literary and theological enterprise was carried out in the 'untrammelled days of Solomon', after the Davidic empire had secured territory to an extent greater than that envisaged even in the more enthusiastic of the age-old promises. When the Yahwist speaks of the past, it is no simple archival matter—in so doing he addresses his contemporaries. Two issues are of vital concern to him: the hiddenness of God's activity in history; and the demonstration in the Davidic period of God's care for Israel. 'If we now read the remarkable conclusion of the Yahwist's work, the lists in Jud. 1, we are at once aware of the relevance which these apparently remote memoranda of territorial history must have had for David's contemporaries and their successors. No one could read these sterotyped descriptions of the as yet unoccupied territories without reflecting that God had not in fact left the matter in this state of semi-fulfilment. He had continued his care for Israel and had kept all his promises, even though it was not in the time of Joshua, but not till in the time of David that this was to be seen. That is what the Yahwist's restrained mode of presentation actually invites us to read between the lines at the end of the work.'[4]

This essay of von Rad certainly achieved its purpose of jolting Hexateuchal studies out of the doldrums. It has received much attention in the intervening period, both enthusiastic and critical. A wholesale re-examination of his case is beyond the scope of this thesis;[5] but certain observations must be made below of those aspects which are fundamental to any consideration of the relationship of the book of Joshua to the Pentateuch. Let it just be noted in conclusion at this stage that when von Rad wrote this essay in 1938, the Hexateuch whose form and growth he sought to explain was a long-established finding of literary scholarship.

B. Noth

(1) *Joshua*

Strikingly, it was also in 1938 that Martin Noth published the first edition of his commentary on Joshua[6]—the first of a series of studies in which he set an emphatic question-mark against this long-established finding. It is to the fifteen-year period of that scholar's career, marked off by the two editions of that commentary, that we must now turn our attention.

At the very beginning of the introduction to his commentary, Noth broaches the problem.[7] Literary critical work on the book had started from the realization that in content the book was but continuation and perhaps completion of the Pentateuch narrative. The taking of Palestine, repeatedly promised, is reported only in this book—and as its main theme. Joshua became associated with the vagaries of Pentateuchal criticism; and the term 'Hexateuch' was resurrected[8] to do better justice to the literary situation now detected. However, various details in the book are counter to its inclusion in study of the Pentateuch—not so much the different kind of origin of much of its material, as that literary critical theses tested principally on the book of Genesis do not hold true in the same evident way for the book of Joshua. The Deuteronomistic[9] redaction, whose extent and style can be easily established, does provide one certain starting-point for our analysis of the book—and the stages following it too can be fairly readily plotted. More difficult to detect is the pre-Deuteronomistic history of the book; but even there, Noth argues, two points may be taken as certain: that before its insertion in the rest Jos. 13:1–21:42 had its own literary history; and that even in the remaining parts of Joshua the literary situation does not resemble that of Genesis. The book's own stock of material must provide the basis for literary analysis, before enquiry is made into pre-Deuteronomistic literary connections with the Pentateuch.

Turning his full attention next to the book's pre-Deuteronomistic history Noth argues first that two documents are the main sources of the section 13:1–21:42—a system of tribal boundaries, and a list of localities in the state of Judah after its division into twelve districts.[10] The combination of these documents served to define the actual property of the twelve tribes in the settlement period—and at this stage without any connection with the Joshua narrative. Out of this description of their actual property grew a description of how under Joshua the land came to be their property;[11] and it was at this stage that the narrative became an integral part of the book of Joshua.

To this pre-Deuteronomistic stage belong also most of the material in Jos. 1–12 and the rudiments of 24. In Chapters 1–12 the Deuteronomist was indebted to an already formed collection, mostly of originally local stories of largely aetiological significance. These once separate stories had been preserved and gathered at the Benjaminite tribal sanctuary of Gilgal, acquiring their all-Israel reference perhaps at the time of Saul when this sanctuary served the people as a whole. These narratives were rounded off by the two hero-stories in chapters 10 and 11. The rudiments of chapter 24 appear to have neither a literary nor a material relationship with the above: the collector has presumably found the basis of this chapter a suitable conclusion.

The new documentary hypothesis declared most of the material in question Elohistic (although *(h)'lhym* as a proper name perhaps does not occur at all)—and Rudolph deemed it Yahwistic, although largely on the negative argument that he found nothing to contradict a derivation from J.[12] Noth makes two points in reply to both: (1) In the Joshua narrative we are dealing with an independent cycle of tradition, in which reference to what has happened previously is made only quite incidentally and quite generally. (2) Even where back-references are made, there is no clear evidence of literary connections with particular narrative sections of the Pentateuch.[13]

It is only with the Deuteronomistic redaction, to which Noth finally devotes himself, that the literary inclusion of the book of Joshua in the entire Hexateuchal (or perhaps better Octateuchal) narrative is demonstrable. This redaction is generally easy to recognize—and in this book as elsewhere it is not homogeneous. In this respect, Noth shows in detail that while chapters 13–21 now appear in a Deuteronomistic framework it is later than that of the rest of the book. The identity of the Deuteronomistic sentences 13:1a and 23:1b is capable of only one interpretation: that 13:1a is a secondary anticipation of 23:1b facilitating the literary incorporation of chapters 13ff.—a repetition in 23:1b, once the statement had already been made in 13:1a, is not a reasonable assumption.

Some portions of the book have a tendency and style similar to the Pentateuchal P. Scholars had long been inclined to attribute to P a large share in 13–21, but these chapters Noth has shown to belong to a secondary Deuteronomistic stage. In fact P's contribution, apart from chapter 21, is just in the form of brief expansions—and so is rather like that of the Deuteronomists: the supplementation of an already existing stock of tradition.

(2) *The Deuteronomist*

Noth's novel approach to Joshua bore as many implications for the study of the Pentateuch as for the study of that book and those immediately surrounding it. And both implications he was quick to tease out in the relevant portions of his researches into those OT historical works produced by the collection and edition of disparate material. In these studies,[14] his main concern is with the Deuteronomistic and Chronistic works; however the implications of his results for the Pentateuch (whose material is a 'collection' only in a limited sense of that term)[15] are presented in an important appendix.

The starting-point in his study of the Deuteronomistic History is 'one of the most assured results of scholarly criticism of the OT'—that in the books from Joshua to Kings we encounter in passages large and small the literary activity of a Deuteronomistic author, so-called because his language and thought exhibit a close relationship with those of the book of Deuteronomy. His language and style are easy to detect throughout, and are testimony to this thesis. But of much greater importance is the fact that the arrangement of the material in these books is the work of the Deuteronomist. The main feature of his edition is that at every important point either the leading actor makes a speech, short or long,[16] or the editor himself offers a comment in his own words[17]—in both cases the course of events is interpreted and the practical conclusions drawn. Such insertions of an author's own reflections have no precise parallel in the OT, and so may be regarded as important evidence for the thesis that the Deuteronomist worked to a unified and compact scheme. A consistent theology is presented; and the unity of his work can be emphasized negatively by comparing with it the multiplicity of the earlier traditions which he uses. Many of these were available in short collections—but the evident unity of the whole familiar corpus is the creation of the Deuteronomistic author alone.

2 Kings 25:27–30 is a natural end to the work; but it is more difficult to agree that Jos. 1 is a natural beginning—it refers back to the history of the Moses period. The common assumption was that the Deuteronomistic historical work had begun with the creation, that it was a stage in the literary growth of the Hexateuch—and that its influence had extended to cover the later historical books. However Noth finds no trace of Deuteronomistic redaction in Genesis to Numbers.[18] Nevertheless, Deut. 31:1–13 and parts of Deut. 34 are elements of a Deuteronomistic narrative to which Jos. 1 is linked; and once this is noted it is soon apparent that Deut. 1:1–4:43 is an introduction not so much to the Deuteronomic Law as to the Deuterononomistic History. It was natural both that our author should

preface his history with an account of the law which was so important to his conception, and that he should present it in the form of a speech by his leading personage.

In the main, Noth's argument in the Joshua commentary confirms and is confirmed by his theory of the Deuteronomistic History. One modification of his earlier conclusions is important for our problem. There is now no mention of any contribution to the book of Joshua from the Pentateuchal source P. Passages such as 21:1–42 and 22:7–34 are now described as additions to the corpus made later than the (itself secondary) inclusion of the bulk of the section 13–22.[19]

Not only does Noth find no trace of the Deuteronomist in the first four books of the Pentateuch, but he also stresses that the Pentateuchal presentation of the early history of Israel—fundamental for faith, and produced essentially by the combination of the sacral Sinai tradition with the equally sacral settlement tradition—was quite different in character from the Deuteronomist's presentation of Israel's history in Palestine. It was only in its introduction that the latter reached back to deal with a few important events in that early history.

Noth was well aware that his thesis once expounded necessitated and (perhaps more positively) enabled a new look to be taken at some of the problems of Pentateuch/Hexateuch. The earlier view that there are literary links between Numbers and Joshua he does not dispute—but he does see them in a new light.[20] This is the stuff of his appendix on the question of P and the redaction of the Pentateuch.[21]

He starts by answering again the question of what part P plays in the composition of the book of Joshua—spelling out the negative results of his commentary conclusions. Those Hexateuchal critics are right who have refused to admit the existence of some small P passages within Jos. 1–12.[22] And in fact this situation is true too of Jos. 13–19. The framework of this section of the book is in three layers, in which the land is divided by the Israelites, Joshua, and a sacral commission respectively. However only the first two of these correspond to the layers of *material* in the book—the pre-Deuteronomistic and the Deuteronomistic. Accordingly, what are at first sight parts of a third framework must be deemed additions to an already existing stock. The basis of Jos. 20 has links with the second framework (appeal is to Joshua alone), and affinities with Deut. 19:1–13. Links with the third 'framework'[23] are obvious in Jos. 21:1–42—with them it must be regarded as an independent addition to the book. And finally 22:9–34,[24] although it resembles P, differs from it in content and language in too many ways for it to be attributed to the Hexateuchal source P. The conclusion: P is nowhere to be found in Joshua—all in all a more radically negative conclusion than that reached in the commentary.

Such a conclusion immediately raises the question of the original extent of P, for the book of Numbers certainly appears to preserve P reports of preparations and commands for the imminent settlement. This Noth now checks in an enquiry into P in Num. 10–36 and Deut. 31–34.

His starting point is important. The last event we know of P describing, if that source is not represented in Joshua, is the death of Moses in Deut. 34:1, 7–9. Of the two preparatory passages, Num. 27:12–14 and Deut. 32:48–52, the latter is demonstrably dependent on the former. Moreover, the closely related Num. 27:15–23—which describes Joshua's commission as Moses' successor—does not refer specifically to his familiar role as occupier and divider of the promised land. It is possible then that the theme of settlement lay outside P's interests. Furthermore, even before Noth, almost all the material recording preparations for the settlement had been generally assigned to secondary parts of the source P. Since these occur for the most part between the announcement of Moses' imminent death in Num. 27 and the far-separated actual record of his death, and since it is possible the settlement lay outside P's interest, Noth felt them worthy of further study.

He first discusses Num. 32–35, whose core he finds in 33:50–34:29. Its kernel in turn is 34:3–12 which lists the boundaries of the land west of the Jordan to be distributed to the tribes. It is based on the same system of boundary description—and so probably the same document too—as that found in Jos. 13–19. Indeed it is most probable that, in the forging of the link between the Deuteronomistic History and the rest of the Pentateuch, the passage in question was transferred to its present position from somewhere in Jos. 13–19—most likely close to 14:1–5. Num. 34:1–2 and also 33:50–51, 54[25] were coined as a new introduction to this boundary description. And since 34:13–15, 16–29 were never deemed part of P's main stock the result is that none of 33:50–34:29 belongs to P. As for Num. 35, vv. 1–8 and 16–34 were generally regarded as late additions to P; and the basic vv. 9–15 Noth argues were composed with Jos. 20 in mind. The situation in Num. 32 is quite different—here J and E make their final appearance in the book of Numbers: vv. 1, 2, 5, 16, 39–42 are a part of their settlement narrative, and the rest of the passage is a secondary expansion of this. As for 33:1–49, it is one of the latest passages in the Pentateuch—and that comment concludes Noth's denial to P of any part of Num. 32–35.

Num. 28–30 and 36 in their turn are generally accepted as being later than the original P. And so, of the material often ascribed to P after Num. 27's announcement of Moses' coming death, only chapter 31 remains to be discussed. Noth admits that if the chapter belongs to one of the major Pentateuchal sources then that source is P—but he questions the hypothesis. Verses 13–54 are a complex of late expansions with no internal unity. And as for 1–12, Noth prefers to agree with Wellhausen and others against von Rad that they are not an original element of the P-narrative—just the first part of a whole chapter that is best described as a supplement to the narrative of the Pentateuch that has formed in successive stages.

Noth turns next to the material in Num. 20–27. The report of the death of Aaron and the appointment of his son Eleazar as successor in 20:22–29 he considers part of the original P. What of the material between this and the commissioning of Joshua? In a separate article on Num. 21 he had already argued that P does not appear in that chapter.[26] Equally there is no sign of it in the Balaam-complex (22:2–24:25). The brief intervening chronological note in 22:1 he does admit as part of P. 25:1–5 is also from one of the earlier sources. As for the remaining complex 25:6–27:11 Noth's conclusion is that it too represents a series of supplements, perhaps five in number, to the basic source material in the Pentateuch—probably intended to fill out the earlier narrative sources, whether before or after the combination of these with P. More certainly they were added before the combination of the Deuteronomistic History with the rest of the Pentateuch—otherwise some of them, and particularly 26:1–54, would have been more likely to be included in the complex 32–35.

As for the material in chapters 10–20, Noth here does not so much challenge the accepted critical results as comment on their significance for his own argument. The spy-story in 13–14 has certainly a necessary connection with the theme of future settlement; but for P the climax of the story is the sin of the spies, except for Joshua and Caleb, and the verdict that a whole generation should die in the desert. P's contribution to the Korah-story in 16–18 seems concerned with the privileges of different priestly factions. (As an omnibus collection of legal prescriptions, chapter 15 has no claim to be considered part of P's narrative. The same is true of chapter 10.) P's share in 20:1–13 again concentrates on culpable lack of faith, this time of Moses and Aaron—it gives the reason for their deaths. And it is noticeable here too, as in the case of the people as a whole in 13–14, that their punishment is really the negative one of not reaching the promised land.

The literary situation at the end of the book of Numbers is then very different from that in the Hexateuch narrative before the Sinai story. But this, Noth observes, is no new conclusion—it was always the first impression of any who came straight from analyzing the primeval and patriarchal histories to take a close look at the literary structure of the second half of Numbers. There one has to deal with a large number of small isolated elements belonging to no major source. These are often reminiscent of P, but they do not belong to its main stock. Even such an attribution as P^s is misleading in that they are, in the main, supplements not to the source P but to the already combined narrative formed of all the major sources.

In the final chapter of this appendix Noth finds it important to stress that P, so far as the total plan of his work was concerned, was content to follow earlier tradition—such as we are familiar with in J. Not that J was necessarily P's literary model—but they both attest the same normative plan. Even the heart of P's concern, the constitution of the Israelite people and cult at Sinai, is narrated within the confines of this long-accepted pattern, despite the lopsidedness of the resultant work. This makes it all the more evident that in his virtual elimination of the settlement theme from his work P is following a quite novel procedure.

It is to this P-work that the final form of the Pentateuch is indebted—this is one of the most certain results of literary criticism. Its first and last words are from P. It is quite as certain that the earlier sources did originally continue to narrate the events of the settlement—verses in Num. 21;32 are evidence of this. How they narrated them must remain in doubt. Old narratives from creation to conquest there had been—but never a 'Hexateuch' in the normal sense of that term, that the books from Genesis to Joshua were once a unity in more or less the form in which we know them.

Their overlap in the matter of the end of Moses' career facilitated the joining of the so-completed Pentateuch to the Deuteronomistic History. Perhaps this join was facilitated by the preservation within the Pentateuch of fragments of the settlement tradition from the earlier sources. This meshing of the two works, themselves complexes of originally separate traditions, helps to explain both the difficult literary situation towards the end of Numbers and how the Pentateuch as we have it still in general gives a relatively ordered impression.

(3) *The Pentateuch*

Just as possibilities opened up by the Joshua commentary were further explored five years later in this study, so after a further five-year period Noth published a full-scale review of the growth of the Pentateuch.[27] His main concern here is with the beginnings of the development of the Pentateuchal traditions—the least worked-over area of Pentateuch criticism. However insofar as a painstaking examination of the Pentateuch's literary problems is a prerequisite of such a study, he prefaces his main work with a summary of his conclusions on this matter.[28]

His comments on P, both in itself and as the literary framework of the whole Pentateuch, mark no advance on what he had already written. His survey of the earlier sources is the more interesting—perhaps in part because the older material is closer to those beginnings of the transmission process which for Noth hold the keys to the whole. These sources are harder to recognize and analyze than P: their language and style are less easily identifiable; violence has been done to their original shape by the discarding, except for traces, of their concluding treatment of the Israelite settlement. It is clear that this earlier material is not a unity—so far, Noth stands in the familiar critical position. But he finds serviceable only one of the familiar criteria for dividing this material: the existence of narrative doublets. And this single criterion proves adequate provided one is clear there should be no preconceived notion that this older material is capable of division into two almost complete *and* almost completely parallel narratives. Many more narratives are a literary unity than is commonly thought; and often only one of the J and E variants of a story will have been preserved. In fact neither E nor J is dependent on the other, but both on a common source of tradition—however, J has been better preserved in the redaction and has been used as the basis for their combination (like P for the Pentateuch).

In the first main chapter of his study of the preliterary development of the stock of constituent traditions, Noth both follows and modifies von Rad's 1938 thesis. In his preface, Noth had already underlined his conviction that the decisive steps on the way to the forming of the Pentateuch were taken at the preliterary stage. And there too he repeated his observation in the *Überlieferungsgeschichtliche Studien*, that unlike the other two OT historical works, the Pentateuch is not merely the result of literary activity—indeed it had no author in the sense that these had: even those responsible for the Pentateuch sources, however important their contribution, cannot be described as authors because they did not give their works their basic shape. This basic shape was not something secondary and supplementary to the originally separate traditions; it was not produced by their being linked to each other. This shape was manifested at the very beginning of the transmission process in a short series of themes which were vital for the faith of the Israelite tribes[29]—themes which were the content of confessions uttered at certain cultic celebrations. These themes were not linked together in one action, but in a gradual process which can still be more or less followed. Here Noth's approach is more complicated than von Rad's. He agrees with the latter that the addition of the primeval history was the last stage in the process; and also that the Sinai story was an originally independent block of tradition only secondarily inserted into what van Rad termed the settlement tradition. However Noth argues that this 'settlement tradition' is itself no original unity. The Pentateuch's tradition of the settlement in Palestine is an independent tradition theme—the Pentateuch as we know it offers no neat join between this theme and the stories of life in the desert and the exodus from Egypt. Even the desert stories are not an independent theme, although a separate one: they function as a link between the themes of preceding exodus and following settlement, and so are subordinate to both. The patriarchal history too is secondary to the following themes; and so the choice for primacy is between exodus and settlement. The two are certainly closely linked; but the former, Noth argues, is more important—and so the prior.

Having established this, he deals in turn with the five themes. And since our immediate concern is with desert and settlement we shall concentrate our view on his comments on these themes. The first theme of exodus is frequently found in the OT quite independently of any other. But it is also often closely followed by the assertion that after Yahweh had brought Israel out of Egypt he then brought it into the land which it thereafter possessed. For all the independence of the first belief, it readily attracted as a conclusion the implicit positive goal of the constitution of a free Israel on its own land. Noth agrees with von Rad that the 'all Israel' reference of this confession was preserved, and indeed perhaps initially achieved, at a common cultic centre. But to give narrative expression to this confession was not without its problems, for there had been no such event as a settlement of Palestine undertaken by Israel as a whole. An 'all Israel' reference was given to the settlement narrative of the tribes of central Palestine—perhaps because at this important stage they controlled the ark and/or the central sanctuary. However, what is certain is that the narrative connection of these two themes was never perfected: the Israelite tribes find themselves suddenly in southern Transjordan having to circumvent Edomite territory to reach their future home; but this is not motivated in the narrative of their rescue from Egypt. This gap is only later and only imperfectly masked by the use of a narrative about a period in the desert, whose stories belong to a quite different original context. As for the theme of patriarchal promise, the development of its narrative tradition was originally quite independent of the rest of the Pentateuch traditions. The element of the promise of land was very important in this body of tradition—indeed it was precisely its prominence that encouraged the mutual assimilation of these traditions and those just discussed—the goal was so similar. The Jacob traditions were probably the first to be represented—they belong to the same central Palestinian area. With the introduction of the majority of the Abraham and Isaac stories we appear to have reached the stage at which southern interests had greater influence on the development of Pentateuchal tradition. This is probably true also of most of the desert material—a contribution of those tribes who had a close connection with the desert country between Egypt and Palestine. Noth commends von Rad's main assumptions about the Sinai traditions, although he adds that his view is not without its problems. This theme too had importance for Israel as a whole; however, its familiar placing within the Pentateuchal traditions is again a contribution of the southern tribes.

Obviously just to state each of these themes required at least a minimum of narrative. Repeated narration led to the increasing of this amount by the addition of any narrative material that had a connection with one of the themes. Most of this development occurred at the stage of oral transmission. Some late pericopes, or at least later reworkings of earlier pericopes, can be detected in which the interests of more than one theme are represented—like the Joseph-story: worth telling for its own sake, and also serving to link both patriarchal and exodus themes. Some genealogies were forged to link the leading personalities in different strands. And then, since the motif of wandering is almost all-pervading in the Pentateuch, itineraries were also used to connect themes and narratives. By this point we are at, or at least close to, the stage of written development. However what is clear is that by the time those responsible for the familiar Pentateuchal 'sources' began their work, the ordering and linking together of the narrative material of the Pentateuch was more or less complete.

The older sources, J and E, both in general and in particular, adhered more faithfully to the given narrative tradition. P was more selective, and felt freer to supplement. Almost as a corollary of this, therefore, J and E left less of a linguistic and stylistic mark on their material than did P—and so were never able to become strictly compact units in a formal sense. Yet each of the sources of the Pentateuch did arrange the given material in its own way in the light of its own particular theological concern.

In his concluding comments, Noth makes one observation which at first sight conflicts with one of his earlier theses. It is important for our topic that we should be clear about his opinion. He urges that if we were to point to a basic theme in the Pentateuch narrative that embraces all the individual themes, it could only be that of the divine leading to Palestine—the divine giving of possession of the land was the red thread amongst the themes forming the creed.[30] Earlier he has written of the theme of deliverance from Egypt that it is (a) the primary confession of all Israel; (b) the kernel of the whole subsequent Pentateuchal tradition; (c) the point of crystallization of the great Pentateuchal narrative in its entirety.[31] Of course relative judgments are hard to make. But is there a conflict here? And how would Noth have reconciled these different comments? Did the exodus tradition provide the first impulse? And then the settlement tradition, once added to it, played a more dominant role—at least in the formation of the Pentateuch?

(4) *Joshua again, and the later commentaries*

Noth's basic contribution to the problem 'Joshua and the Pentateuch' was completed a further five years later, with the publication in 1953 of the second edition of his commentary on Joshua. Insights won in his two major studies of Israel's traditions are now employed in a thorough recasting of the introduction to the commentary, whose first version had been an important stage in the whole endeavour.

In the first section of the introductory chapter only the odd word or phrase is added or altered, to strengthen the already present emphasis on the necessity of viewing the book of Joshua, at least in the first instance, quite separately from the Pentateuch and its peculiar problems. However, the exposition of the book's construction starts now not with its pre-Deuteronomistic history but with a treatment of the Deuteronomistic book itself—for the Deuteronomistic stage is the one most easily identified and compared with other neighbouring books in the canon. Naturally the basis for discussion now is Noth's own theory of the Deuteronomistic Historical Work, with no further talk of any inclusion of the pre-Deuteronomistic material in a Deuteronomistic Hexateuch or Octateuch. This Deuteronomistic book is shown to have been produced in two stages: the first is framed by 1:1–18 on the one hand and 21:43–22:6 and 23:1–16 on the other; the other consists of the two additions 13:1–21:42 and 24. Later additions are now listed, much as in the previous edition.[32] Only then is the pre-Deuteronomistic history of the book discussed, again with changes of structure: chapter 24 is now discussed quite separately from chapters 1–12;[33] and the question of literary connections between this material and the Pentateuch sources is assigned to a section on its own.

In subsequent commentaries on Exodus, Leviticus, and Numbers,[34] Noth both amplified and modified many details of this massive contribution to 'Hexateuchal' studies just reviewed. Two details relating to the final chapters of Numbers may serve to illustrate this and also contribute to our topic. Num. 34:3–12 is not now considered to have been transposed from Jos. 14, but is stated to have been composed on the basis of information about boundaries contained in Jos. 15–19.[35] And the treatment of the early sources in Num. 32 also differs from his earlier position. It is now stated that vv. 39–42 are from a quite independent source; and that, while there can be no certainty as to whether the early material in vv. 1–38 is from one or both of the early sources, it is likely that J has contributed v. 1 and perhaps also vv. 16–19.[36]

C. Von Rad and Noth

Two reviews of Noth by von Rad repay our attention. The first, entitled 'Hexateuch oder Pentateuch?',[37] observes with appreciation that the question of the Hexateuch hypothesis could have been broached at no more fortunate point than the book of Joshua. He finds Noth's exposition of the extent of P and its original content plausible—but observes that just as his theses are difficult to prove, so too are they difficult to refute in any exact way. He is concerned to know where a critical method describing parts of the end of Numbers as secondary additions derived from parts of Joshua which are themselves in turn secondary additions to that book will call a halt. Yet he is certain that the necessary refutation will not be achieved by purely literary-critical methods. Noth's problems are real ones; yet *may* a Pentateuchal source be operated on so incisively without a more exact knowledge of its internal nature, of its actual theological intention? It is not wrong to work on the basis of a hypothesis which is only confirmed in the course of the operation—but could Noth have denied to P passages such as Num. 34:1–12 had his own conception of P not obtruded more and more? Von Rad would clearly be pleased if a sound method were to come to hand to challenge the one-sidedness *he* detects in Noth's statement that 'it is not the literary state of affairs which must be determined by a particular view of P, but rather our view of P which must be determined by the literary state of affairs'. If it is to correct conclusions that this methodological one-sidedness has led Noth then the form-critical connection between the credo in Deut. 26 and (at least) P would have to be abandoned—of that von Rad is convinced.[38]

The critique is continued in his article 'Literarkritische und überlieferungsgeschichtliche Forschung im Alten Testament'.[39] Here his reading of Noth's account of the development of the Pentateuch prompts two main questions. The first is whether or not Noth's 'themes' represent a stage preliminary to that of the credo. Here he does not offer a direct answer to his own question, but merely notes the possibility of the assumption that even after their combination in the credo the individual themes would have preserved an independent existence. (Later, in the first volume of his *Old Testament Theology*, he did comment on Noth's view of their independence: 'The literary material seems to justify him, for in the majority of cases the "themes" seem to be independent. Nevertheless these single themes themselves always presuppose an idea of the whole.')[40] Von Rad's second point is difficult to deal with in English or German; but it is related to this first question, and so is important for our problem. He asks if Noth has not described the process of the growing together of the traditions in too formal a way. And he links this to Noth's use of the term 'tradition' (*Überlieferung*) too in a dominantly formal way. Admitting that the point he is to make is one of emphasis only, he states that the important thing about a unit of tradition (*Überlieferung*) is not so much that it has had such and such a history and has achieved such and such a form, but that it belongs to such and such a sacral or theological stream or current of tradition which is similar to or divergent from other such currents of tradition. Invoking the distinction between *Überlieferung* and *Tradition*,[41] he suggests that a *Traditionsgeschichte* might be more useful than an *Überlieferungsgeschichte* as a tool for studying the Pentateuch/Hexateuch—and particularly for studying the P-complex within it.

Von Rad appears to overstate his case here: in principle both quests would be appropriate. This debate between Noth and von Rad is at the same time instructive and hard to assess. Perhaps the main point at issue between them is a different emphasis on the tenacity of form. There is a tension discernible in Noth's writing between his respect for von Rad's case on the one hand and the more complicated point he wants to make on the other.[42] Von Rad's essay appears to have been Noth's inspiration rather than his blueprint. The two scholars agree that there is a striking similarity between the shape of the old credo and the shape of the Pentateuch or Hexateuch.[43] But Noth finds no straight line of development from the one to the other. Rather is it the case that those themes (that reflected the constitution of the people and their faith), whose common subject encouraged their fusion in the old cultic credo, also grew together—decked with much narrative embellishment—in a quite separate process and then continued accumulating material until they were finally given literary form by the authors of the earliest sources of the Pentateuch. Noth assents to the idea of the tenacity of form—witness his account of P's development of his Sinai material *within* the inherited schema. Yet his treatment of P's handling of the settlement theme shows that this concept of form has no absolute status for him. However it is not only his attitude on this matter that appears freer than von Rad's. He also has a different starting-point: not the old credo of Deut. 26:5–9 (perhaps shorn of a few Deuteronomic embellishments), but the exodus confession.

In 1938 it was an assured result of literary criticism that all the main sources of the Pentateuch were to be found also in Joshua.[44] Von Rad's essay of that year offered an attractive explanation of this given literary situation. Noth's series of studies rendered this literary conclusion at the least questionable.[45]

Von Rad's 1938 essay assumes the literary-critical conclusion of a Hexateuch. It does not argue for it—nor should it, *on its own*, be cited in support of it. It may be his realization of this that prompts von Rad's supplementary and *a priori* assumption concerning the tenacity of form and the conservatism of tradition. Yet such an assumption is as hard to refute as to prove, and so is subject to the very critique that von Rad directed against Noth.[46]

And yet—has Noth not conceded too much to von Rad's thesis? Granted (a) that the desert material is largely from an original milieu different from that of the settlement traditions, and (b) that (in Noth's latest published view) the ascription to J of even four verses (Num. 32:1, 16–19) on the settlement theme is only *probable*, it is difficult to believe that he has heeded his own strictures—on the question of P and the settlement—of paying attention first to the literary situation. Surely these four verses, taken for themselves, could have been more satisfactorily explained as part of the complicated redactional situation Noth has himself disclosed in Num. 27–36.

Both von Rad and Noth see the settlement theme as the goal of the Pentateuch/Hexateuch. It may be that Noth's literary-critical considerations make his own case no less doubtful than von Rad's. The legitimacy of adducing the Deuteronomic credos in the discussion is very questionable.[47] They fit their own context well: the themes of desert wandering and settlement correspond to narrative sections in the books of Deuteronomy and Joshua; and those of the fathers and of deliverance from Egypt are frequently referred to in the same books.[48]

Such criticism is negative. It demands as a positive counterpart the furnishing of an alternative rationale for the development of the Pentateuch—but that is beyond the confines of this thesis. Only one footnote may be offered; Noth argued that it was their common interest in the granting of the land which made reasonable in the first place the prefixing of the patriarchal theme to that of the settlement. But at the same time he admitted that there is much material in the patriarchal complex in the Pentateuch which has no direct reference to the question of the land. It would be instructive to pursue the latter observation further, and reconsider the question whether it was this element in the material (central or not) that facilitated its connection with other parts of the Pentateuch traditions.

However Noth's literary conclusions have been fundamentally criticized by Mowinckel (amongst others). Accordingly it is to his contribution to the debate that we must now turn our attention.

NOTES

1. Translated in *Problem of the Hexateuch*, pp. 1–78.
2. *Prolegomena*, pp. 342ff.
3. *Le Décalogue* (1927).
4. It is striking that von Rad makes no mention of any J-material between the Balaam cycle and Jud. 1.
5. Nicholson's *Exodus and Sinai* is a useful more recent contribution to the debate; earlier studies are conveniently cited and reviewed there.
6. *Das Buch Josua* (1938).
7. *op. cit.*, pp. VII, VIII. In fact Noth's first brief section is on the text of Joshua: he finds that the Hebrew text has been well preserved, and that the LXX (while occasionally representing a more original Hebrew text) results in the main from simplifications to a Hebrew text itself the product of a complicated literary history.
8. This term, and also 'Heptateuch', 'Octateuch' and 'Enneateuch' (referring to the books up to Judges, Samuel and Kings) were used by early Fathers of the Church.
9. In this part of our study, Noth's own usage is followed: the adjective Deutero*nomic*, for what belongs to the book of Deuteronomy; and the adjective Deutero*nomistic*, for anything pertaining to the narrative of the Deuteronomists, who were themselves influenced by Deuteronomy. Partly because Noth's own studies detected Deuteronomistic influence on the book of Deuteronomy itself, some have found this distinction problematic and have preferred to use but one adjective, Deuteronomic, rather ambiguously. Evidence of both usages will be found later in this volume.
10. This case he had already stated more fully in *ZDPV* 58, pp. 185ff., a series of essays themselves indebted to studies by Alt—see *KS* II, pp. 276ff.; *KS* I, pp. 193ff.; and *ZAW* 45, pp. 59ff.
11. Noth claims that there are still traces in Jos. 14:1a, 4a, 5; and 19:49a of a stage in the tradition in which it was the Israelites themselves who took the land for their own possession.
12. *Der 'Elohist' von Exodus bis Joshua.*
13. Noth does remark that in some respects his view of the pre-Deuteronomistic history of these sections of the book is not unlike the essential elements of Rudolph's view, in which too there is the assumption of a basic narrative which has been subsequently expanded in successive stages.
14. *Überlieferungsgeschichtliche Studien I* (1943).
15. Quoting von Rad's 1938 essay as a crucial account of the growth of the Pentateuch, he observes that despite the wealth of historical detail in the Pentateuch, its subject-matter is really a set of particular given themes which are fundamental for faith.

16. Jos. 1; 23; 1 Sam. 12; 1 Kings 8:14ff. McCarthy, in his essay on 'II Samuel 7', makes a powerful case for adding that speech too to Noth's list.
17. Jos. 12; Jud. 2:11ff.; 2 Kings 17:7ff.
18. Passages such as Ex. 23:20ff. and 34:10ff., in which an early text has been expanded in Deuteronomistic style, are not evidence for Noth of continuous redaction.
19. Contrast *UGS*, p. 45, n. 4 with *Josua*[1], p. XIV. There is some inconsistency over Noth's treatment of Jos. 21: in the introduction to the commentary he describes chapters 13–21 as a main section of the book of Joshua; and in this study, chapters 13–22. However in both works, 21 (and 22 too) is dealt with quite separately from the section to which it is said to belong.
20. Earlier Hexateuchal critics had considered the relevant parts of Joshua to belong to the same source as, and to narrate the carrying out of the commands described in, the related parts of Numbers.
21. *UGS*, pp. 180–217.
22. For example, 4:15–17, 19; 5:10–12; 9:14, 15b, 17–21.
23. 14:1b; 18:1; 19:51a.
24. Jos. 21:43–22:6(8) is a part of the Deuteronomistic redaction.
25. The verses 52, 53, 55, 56 are generally described as secondary.
26. *ZAW* 58, pp. 161ff. Noth's exposition of this chapter confirms and amplifies two basic points: (i) that it occupies a bridge position in the 'Hexateuch' (from this point onwards he regularly uses this term in quotation marks), the centre of interest moving from the desert to the settlement; (ii) that its literary composition is typical of the latter part of Numbers as a whole, where most of the evidence supports a supplementary rather than a documentary hypothesis.
27. *Überlieferungsgeschichte des Pentateuch* (1948), cited here as *HPT*, in its English translation. Noth's use in this study, as in the previous one, of the term 'Pentateuch' is somewhat misleading in that it regularly refers to that entity formed by the insertion of the older sources into the P-framework, and hence does not include Deuteronomy. It was Engnell who coined the term 'Tetrateuch'.
28. *HPT*, pp. 5–41.
29. That is, their common faith: Noth had already expounded in one of his earliest studies, *Das System* (1930), his view that the 12-tribe Israelite system was not formed before the settlement in Palestine. That then is the *terminus a quo* for the development of the 'all-Israelite' Pentateuch tradition.
30. *op. cit.*, p. 191.
31. *op. cit.*, p. 49—cf. also p. 190.
32. Jos. 21:1–42 is now (*Josua*[2], p. 15) discussed explicitly in the context of 13:1–21:42 (cf. above p. 6 and n. 19).
33. Noth's opinion in the first edition was that the Deuteronomist had composed chapter 23 on the pattern of the core of chapter 24, which itself was one section of the traditional material which he reworked (p. XIII). But in *UGS* (p. 9, n. 1) he repudiated both parts of this view, and argued that the originally independent core of chapter 24 was reworked in Deuteronomistic style and inserted into the completed work at a place appropriate for an important contribution to the history of Joshua.
34. Published as numbers 5, 6, 7 of the ATD in 1959, 1962, 1966.
35. *Numbers* (1968), pp. 248–249.
36. *op. cit.*, pp. 234–241.
37. *VuF* (1949/50), pp. 52ff.
38. Von Rad was, perhaps, particularly interested and worried by Noth's conclusions about P, having himself published in 1934 *Die Priesterschrift im Hexateuch*. His attempt there to divide the basic core of P into two strata found very little acceptance, and he tacitly abandoned the view.

39. *VuF* (1949/50), pp. 172ff.
40. *OTTh* I, p. 122, n. 21.
41. The distinction is more or less than between 'unit of tradition' and 'body of tradition', or between '*a* tradition' and '*T*radition'.
42. Noth regularly gives the impression in his work of having sought common ground where he could do so without compromise.
43. Or, more particularly, the shape of J and E, its earliest literary sources.
44. The studies on the 'Elohist' by Volz and Rudolph (1933) and Rudolph alone (1938) represent no exception to this.
45. Von Rad goes some way to conceding this in *OTTh* I, p. 298, n. 4.
46. See above, p. 13.
47. There is no parallel within Genesis-Numbers to any of these credos.
48. Rost, in the title essay of his collection *Das kleine Credo*, pp. 11–25, has demonstrated that there are more Deuteronomistic additions to the credo in Deut. 26 than von Rad realized in 1938. Von Rad is believed to have conceded this point also. For other relevant discussions, see Nicholson, *Exodus and Sinai*, pp. 20–21.

CHAPTER II

MOWINCKEL AND NOTH

A. Mowinckel

(1) *Introductory*

Mowinckel's most important work in the area of our topic is his monograph *Tetrateuch-Pentateuch-Hexateuch*, published in 1964 at the end of an almost fifty-year long publishing career. His main scholarly interest lay in the interpretation of the Psalms, and in particular the evidence they provided for an evaluation of hitherto unnoticed aspects of Israel's cultic life. Yet, although it was not his central concern, he had always taken an interest in the literary problems of the Pentateuch and in the associated questions about the early history of Israel and the growth of her traditions. It may in fact be misleading to consider the above-mentioned monograph a product of Mowinckel's final years—(a) there is some evidence to suggest that at least its chapter on J was in manuscript in his native Norwegian by the mid 1940s;[1] (b) and what is certain is that the work takes account only of the first edition of Noth's commentary on Joshua and his *Überlieferungsgeschichtliche Studien* of 1943.[2]

(2) *Three Post-War Studies*

There is little if any evidence in Mowinckel's earlier writings for an independent position on the general problem of the growth and structure of the Pentateuch.[3] But important elements of his later quite distinctive attitude to these problems were worked out in three significant studies published soon after the Second World War.

The main purpose of the first of these, *Prophecy and Tradition* (1946), is to study the nature of Israel's prophetic tradition; and this is treated in its second half. However, first Mowinckel examines appropriateness in method for our approach to the study of Israel's traditions of all kinds; and comments on the group of questions suggested by the phrases form criticism, tradition criticism, literary criticism, oral tradition, and literary tradition. The fairly early recognition in the history of OT scholarship that the earliest stage in the process of transmission had been an oral popular tradition meant that at least de facto a traditio-historical approach had long been used beside the literary one.[4] Their relationship was seldom discussed in principle. Mowinckel declares himself opposed to those who use the term tradition criticism almost as a slogan, and in conscious opposition to literary criticism. Engnell, representing the final phase of the traditio-historical point of view, proclaimed his approach as consistently traditio-historical. He did not define this phrase; but his work is notable for two emphases: that the formation and transmission of the OT material was in principle by word of mouth;[5] and that this process of growth makes it dangerous in principle to probe behind the tradition as it now exists—motif analysis and the search for strata are usually in vain. Mowinckel finds it possible to assent to the first of Engnell's axioms without conceding that the second follows with any logical necessity. And he notes that Engnell's refusal to try to penetrate into the origin and history of the tradition is difficult to reconcile with his own slogan 'consistently traditio-historical'. He agrees that earlier discussion of OT literature had assumed the material to be too 'literary', and had reckoned too much with written works even in early Israelite times. However 'Nyberg's—in itself valuable—point of view[6] cannot tell us anything of importance about the *real history of the tradition*—and that is just what we want to know something about.'[7]

The third of these post-war studies,[8] a critique of Pedersen's handling of Ex. 1–15 as the cult-legend of the Passover festival,[9] offers Mowinckel the opportunity of a specific rebuttal of the view that tradition-history is an exclusive alternative to literary criticism. To counter Pedersen's approach, he states and defends several theses: In its present form, Ex. 1–15 is conceived as an integral part of a historical work. Despite their basis in a cult legend, these chapters contain much material of a different kind. The many unevennesses—admitted by Pedersen—are so numerous and can be linked together so readily that Mowinckel is content to stand in the long critical tradition which claims that they belong to at least one separate and consistent strand parallel to the 'main line' detected by Pedersen. The inconsistencies are both narrative and theological—these correspond both with each other and with similar strands elsewhere in the Pentateuch.[10]

The second of these three studies[11] relates directly to Noth's handling of Jos. 13–19, and provoked a specific response from him[12]—it will be convenient to deal with these together. It is Mowinckel's view that P (a post-exilic Jerusalemite historian) was the author—and not just compiler or redactor—of Jos. 13–19; but he is not to debate this—rather whether and how far the author used earlier documents among his sources. His detailed criticism is directed almost entirely at the studies of Alt and Noth on these chapters.[13] He agrees with Alt[14] that the lists of cities of Judah, Benjamin, Simeon, and Dan[15] represent the situation in Josiah's Judah, that they are not consistent with the descriptions of boundaries in Jos. 15–19, and that a Josian document listing them could conceivably have once existed. However, he is convinced that such a document would not have survived the firing of temple and palace in 587; and is unable to understand what purpose oral preservation of an administrative list reflecting a now antiquated situation could have served in the post-exilic period. Aspirations aroused by Josiah's successes would still have been alive in post-exilic Jerusalem; and his administrative areas would have survived to some extent even in the smaller Persian province of Judah. And so the necessary knowledge could have been preserved without the possession or even memory of a list. Furthermore, that P in giving his more or less accurate list of cities came into conflict with his much more idealistic boundaries for the old tribes is not difficult to understand.

The explanation by Alt and Noth of the system of tribal boundaries also draws his attack. Noth's argument that different descriptions in Joshua of the same boundary imply a basic list of towns variously filled out he counters by suggesting that the situation is better explained by assuming stylistic variation in the original version, and one or two scribal mistakes in the subsequent transmission of the text! Furthermore, as to the pre-monarchic tribal system appealed to by Alt and Noth as arbiter—on the basis of these lists—in border disputes, he has two comments to make: (1) such system as there was had inadequate political power for such a role; and (2) in any case the pre-monarchic system was of only ten tribes. In fact the concrete assertions in Jos. 13–19 about boundaries reproduce traditions and facts from different periods which it is not always possible to separate and which are of very different worth.

Unlike J (in Jud. 1), P had assumed that the whole of Palestine had been conquered by Israel under Joshua, and that since then it had belonged to Israel justly and in God's eyes. Proceeding as he did from actual knowledge of the situation in his time, P faced insurmountable problems when he came to deal with Simeon and Dan: he knew nothing about their borders in the early period; they no longer existed as tribes in the areas where he knew they had lived in the period of the settlement—all he did know was that they had lived in areas which had for a long time since lain within the boundaries of Judah and Ephraim. However this incongruence between his theory and the actual state of his knowledge is no basis for imagining the existence of an old system of tribal boundaries which had assigned clear boundaries to each of the tribes.

Having stated that Jos. 13–19 is the natural solution by the author P to the problem facing him, Mowinckel attempts to consolidate his position by meeting in advance any objection that only through documents could he have had information about boundaries in the early period. Tradition, he states, was more important than documents. At an early period the tribes had become geographical rather than ethnological concepts, and so popular knowledge of divisions had lived on long after these divisions had ceased to have any administrative significance. Information about a whole country transmitted in such a way is liable to contain quite contradictory details—such discrepancy is no evidence for the use of written sources.

He does agree with Alt and Noth (and indeed most researchers) that the fact that much more information is given in these chapters about the southern than about the northern tribes provides a basis for drawing some conclusions about the date and place of their composition. The interest is Judaean—and almost Jewish. The treatment of Ephraim and Manesseh in 16–17 supports this view: even less interest is taken in them than in the tribes further north—and that this section is connected with P is clear from the fact that 17:2–6 is based on P's information about Manesseh in Num. 26:28–34. Noth is certainly right that the author is not the Deuteronomist; but, despite Noth, the author's post-exilic Jewish outlook confirms the assumption that he was in fact P.

In his concluding comments, Mowinckel underlines his agreement with Alt about two obvious attributes of the tribal system of these chapters: its theoretical character, according to which the whole country within its ideal boundaries had been overcome all at once under Joshua and distributed in its entirety amongst the tribes; and the importance to its author of adhering to what he knew of the historical realities and of the traditions and popular opinions. However he is satisfied that Alt's and Noth's source hypotheses do not stand up to close examination. In terms of the history of scholarship they have to be considered as the final relics of a dictatorship of pure literary criticism. The results of this documentary approach are only ostensibly assured and concrete. Mowinckel's own advocated approach on the basis of tradition history produces results less illusory and more modest—we must be content with a wealth of detail from the early period, and only a rough picture of the situation.

B. Noth: a Response

Noth's reply[16] to this opens with some general comments on the difficulty of coming adequately to terms with such a complex and anonymous mass of material as is our Old Testament—comments entirely in the spirit of Mowinckel's own observations in *Prophecy and Tradition*.[17] Turning to Jos. 13–21, he notes that it has been generally assumed that the long lists of names in these chapters are not suited to oral transmission. Not surprisingly he utterly rejects Mowinckel's protest that his and Alt's studies of these chapters evidence a purely literary-critical dictatorship in scholarship. They are somewhat removed from the general literary-critical analysis of the book of Joshua, their interest being centred on the actual *material* of the book and its history. And in any case, he asks, is Mowinckel not inconsistent in his charge when he himself opens his study with the assumption (taken over from literary criticism) that the section's author was the hypothetical P of Pentateuchal criticism?

He rejects Mowinckel's argument about the catastrophe of 587, for it is an incontrovertible fact that written records did survive Judah's downfall. When the books of Kings refer to written annals, they *could* be meaning collections made from the royal annals only after 587. But this material must have been available in writing—at some stage of its literary transmission it must have survived the calamity. And other non-official material already committed to writing before the Assyrian and Babylonian campaigns had also survived them. Accordingly the enquiry into Jos. 13–19 must confine itself to internal considerations. Noth does not doubt competence to remember and transmit lists of hundreds of names, but finds—in a period in which writing served several purposes—Mowinckel's assumption a case of 'oral tradition at any price' taken to the extreme. On the other hand, Mowinckel does not make clear just to what extent 'tradition' is present in Jos. 13–19—he has stressed that a good deal of the system worked out by the author P derives from his own knowledge of the land and his 12-tribe theory. Mowinckel's literary-critical assumption about P as the author must also be tested against an actual traditio-historical examination of these chapters really based on their contents, and not against the entirety of 'Hexateuchal' scholarship.[18] And this is particularly necessary since he has rejected those findings of recent years which have developed from the text of the chapters and not from a theory foisted upon them.

Mowinckel agrees that the boundary descriptions represent an essentially complete whole—but one worked out by P. Noth is doubtful whether the detail and exactness of these chapters do speak for a late date. The various administrative and political reorganizations had reduced the relevance of precise demarcations of tribal boundaries; and so it is hardly likely that a late author would have developed as precise a system as we find in Jos. 13–19. Yet Mowinckel *has* posed a relevant question regarding the 'Sitz im Leben' of a boundary system before the formation of the state. Without offering any further substantiation, Noth remarks that a 12-tribe system is the earliest form of organization in Israel which we can detect, and that there is evidence for it before the formation of the state. If the league is to be thought of as functioning in any sense as a community, then any boundary problems must have been solved otherwise than by the law of the stronger. If a more concrete solution is desirable, then one could look to the institution of the 'Judges of Israel'.[19]

Despite the fact that Noth's preamble could have been written by either scholar, their two arguments do not really engage with each other at some important points—such as the effect of the physical destruction in 587 on the preservation of Israel's traditions, and whether the earliest detectable form of Israelite organization is a 10-tribe or 12-tribe league. Yet both admit that they are grappling with a very complex problem; both argue that the complexities have been made greater here and there by textual corruptions and/or editorial alterations subsequent to the completion of the main body of the text. However a final answer to this question must await both a more detailed review of Jos. 13–19 and a fuller discussion of Pentateuchal criticism.

A. MOWINCKEL (CONTD.)

(3) *Israelite Historiography*

It is in three studies published in his last years that we find Mowinckel's mature contribution to our problem as a whole.[20] The first of these is an important and concise statement about the development of historical traditions in Israel,[21] and embodies a critique mainly of Hölscher[22] and Noth. He is particularly concerned to refute Hölscher's claim that J (whose saga runs from creation to the disruption after Solomon) was the first Israelite historian. Mowinckel agrees that J belongs after the disruption, and probably not before 800 B.C., but finds that his skill, and the great synthesis he offers, show he was scarcely Israel's first historian. In fact the first mentioned written source of the Deuteronomist is the 'History of Solomon' (1 Kings 11:41), which clearly cannot have been identical with the 'Annals of the Kings of Judah and Israel' quoted elsewhere. Rost and von Rad are correct that a central element in this oldest history was concern for the legitimacy of the Solomonic line on the throne of David—its extent had been most of what we read in 1 Kings 1–10. The next stage in the expanding history had been the prefixing of more details about David—and since his youth was inextricably bound up with the careers of Saul and Samuel, and since it had been the policy of David and his supporters to appear as the legitimate heir of Saul, 1 Sam. 1 is a natural beginning for this expanded Solomon saga. The combination and 'theologization' of the old traditions of Exodus, Sinai and settlement was a process partly older than this literary activity, partly parallel to it, and partly independent of it. As with this historical activity just described it took place in the circles of the learned men at court and in the sanctuary, and also among the wandering *homines religiosi* and story-tellers. Von Rad has correctly drawn the broad lines of this traditio-historical process that culminated in the work of J. This saga-writer is not, as Hölscher thinks, the first Israelite historian; but he did write something like a religious philosophy of history, to which later Israelite historiography was much indebted. His history has connections with ideas of his own time: it points forward to the glories of the Davidic state; its polemic against the cult of the ox image at Bethel shows that J worked after the disruption. The conclusion of J (at least in an expanded form) was one of the Deuteronomist's sources of his history of Israel. It is a problem to know how he had access to all this earlier historiography after the destruction of the archives in 587. There had never been many manuscripts of the books mentioned above; but we must remember that among the 'remnant of Israel' there must have been men who more or less knew the old literature by heart. As Nyberg has shown, the catastrophe of 587 with its attendant fear of the rapid extinction of the traditions was the occasion for a more systematic writing down of all knowledge considered important to society. The Deuteronomistic saga demonstrates to what a degree the history of the people was considered to be of religio-pedagogical value for the life of the community.

(4) *Pentateuchal Sources*

The second of these final studies of Mowinckel consists of a series of reflections on the Pentateuch source question.[23] Not surprisingly its contents overlap considerably those of *Tetrateuch-Pentateuch-Hexateuch*—and so here only its distinctive contribution will be reviewed. Mowinckel first turns his attention to P in the Pentateuch,[24] and begins by answering Löhr[25] and Volz[26] who had explained the familiar P-passages as expansions of the earlier historical work (JE). He notes with approval Rudolph's subsequent disagreement with his colleague Volz: although the revision-hypothesis is a likely one for Deut. 34:1–9 and Jos. 14–19, yet in Exodus and Numbers there is a series of P-passages which are real narratives. The final proof that P is an independent Pentateuch source, and not a series of insertions made by the final Pentateuch editor, is his quite explicit theory about the use of different divine names at different stages in the prehistory. Had he been the redactor of the old traditions he would have been bound to re-edit the patriarchal stories in accordance with his theory. It is a principal characteristic of P that his work is a combination of historical presentation and of ritual law. This author was really a narrator; but his presentation of history constitutes only the frame round the laws, and in many cases is only an introductory notice about the motive for this or that law. Mowinckel suggests that P did not so much write the early history of his people as its early church history. Wellhausen's opinion is unexceptionable that at almost every point P is directly or indirectly dependent on JE, and with few exceptions represents the latest stage of the development of the material found in J.[27]

When one has separated off the P-source from the rest of the Pentateuch, it is methodologically appropriate to treat what remains as a unity—at least provisionally. Scholars agree that some distinction must be drawn between the whole extent of these remains and the original J—it is an examination of this original J that Mowinckel next offers. It is now generally recognized, he claims, that the material absorbed by J consisted of independent narratives and narrative complexes. Noth's contribution to this field of study is particularly valuable; yet Mowinckel admits to some misgivings about his classification by themes—as modern and systematic, and making insufficient allowance for the 'genetic' development of traditions. On the other hand he finds no difficulty with the idea of points of crystallization. He is also unhappy with the view that the desert theme (about whose independence he has grave doubts) is the cradle in which the Sinai theme now lies. Mowinckel denies von Rad's claim that it was J who first collected the separate themes together—Noth's postulated G is valid to the extent that there was a more or less integrated body of tradition available to J. However von Rad is probably correct that it was J who first committed the traditions to writing. He agrees with both that J did include some kind of report of the settlement.

The second half of this book Mowinckel devotes to an examination of the problem of the Elohist. At many points a division has been made between J and E only because in other cases scholars had been convinced of the existence of two sources.[28] Mowinckel discusses four blocks of material which are examples of an ungrounded separation between J and E by traditional literary criticism: the Primeval History;[29] the Joseph story; the Jacob narratives; and Ex. 1–15—even the famous passage Ex. 3:11–14 with its explanation of the name of Yahweh gives no cause for a separation into parallel sources. And yet there are passages in the older story known to P which a redactor has composed from two parallel strands or doublets: the Sinai pericope; the Balaam story[30]—and Gen. 20:1–17; and 21:8–34 are clearly foreign bodies within the original J cycle of narratives about Abraham, as too is 15:1–6.

His final two examples of passages in the earlier saga where parallel strands have been combined are of particular importance to the problem 'Joshua and Pentateuch'. Since their treatment in this study differs somewhat from that in the following one, what Mowinckel has to say here should now be reviewed. The first passage is Num. 32.[31] Apart from some 'Deuteronomizing' additions the narrative is a unity—with the important exception of vv. 39, 41, 42. The main part of the chapter is a late compilation; but the verses at the end are of a quite different kind, and it is clear that they rather than the main part of the chapter belong to J. Verse 40 is redactional—it picks up v. 39[32] but sees the matter from another point of view. It is possible that the main story in the chapter has suppressed notices about Reuben and Gad corresponding to those about Machir/Manasseh in the concluding verses—remains of these may be detected in vv. 1, 4–5, 34–38. Mowinckel's conclusion is that the old J-report has been expanded by the inclusion of a longer narrative which itself is only a development of historical motifs found in J.

The other passage is the report of the conquest in Jos. 2–11. Jud. 1 was the original concluding passage of J's saga; J had no historical tradition with which to write a history of the conquest—but he did offer a geographically arranged review of its results. Traditional literary criticism assumed that in Jos. 1–11 the Deuteronomist had built on an older source which was identified as the combined JE. Mowinckel notes that the geographical arrangement of these chapters is the same as that in Jud. 1, and argues that they were composed on its plan, and to replace it. This later account was combined with the original J—or more precisely parts of the latter were inserted in it—and then J's review was made the conclusion of the whole account[33] (for which it is as unsuitable as could be!). If J told at all of the crossing of the Jordan and the first taking of a piece of the promised land, then it may be safely assumed that he reported the old tradition of the taking of Jericho which we find in Jos. 2; 6:25. The remainder of chapter 6 is a spiritless priestly story—and this situation in chapters 2 and 6 demonstrates that in Jos. 2–11 too a later narrative has been combined with J's account.[34]

None of these additional sections to the earlier narrative of the Pentateuch provides evidence of a separate parallel source 'E'—they do show that the material collected and written down by J did continue to develop and expand orally. However, with the exception of the story of the settlement, no material was later added to J which already in more original form was not part of J—and even the settlement story had its plan provided by J.

(5) *Tetrateuch-Pentateuch-Hexateuch*

And this leads us naturally to Mowinckel's final and most explicit contribution to our problem.[35] In a brief opening survey of the history of scholarly opinion about the Pentateuch/Hexateuch problem, he describes both Wellhausen's classic lead to Hexateuchal criticism and the equally successful later demonstration by Noth and Engnell[36] that the Deuteronomist's work begins only with Deuteronomy. It is Noth's (and Engnell's) subsequent conclusions he is to examine—and in particular whether J and P told of the settlement and what they told. He repeats briefly the results of the previous study that while P was an independent narrator, 'E' represents only a piecemeal development of the tradition represented by J —the resultant form of the tradition being best represented symbolically as J^v (i.e. 'Jahwista variatus').

In the first main chapter Mowinckel deals with the Yahwist's report of the settlement. He draws on von Rad's work, and states that it is clear from its very beginning[37] that the whole of J's composition has as its goal Israel's occupation of the land promised to the fathers—it must have actually described this. Even Noth admits that—the only question is whether J's report is available to us. Turning first to Num. 32, he first remarks that at least here in the Pentateuch it is universally admitted that elements of an earlier saga are to be found in an otherwise secondary tradition-formation. As a whole, it is a late tradition—nothing actually happens in the chapter: it is clearly an aetiological explanation of the familiar situation of the settlement of Reuben, Gad and half-Manasseh. However the final verses (39–42)[38] are very different, and preserve the historical recollection that the Manassite clan Machir had occupied Gilead from west of the Jordan. These verses are elements of J's report of the settlement. Moving to the book of Joshua he argues that within Jos. 1–11 (which as a whole is the Deuteronomistic report of the conquest) there are traces of earlier traditions—and it is reasonable to suppose that these had been part of the only early story of the conquest known to us, i.e. J's, of which traces have been found in Num. 32. The passages in question are 2; 6:25; and 11:13. In the second half of the book too there are notices of an anecdotal character similar to those already mentioned.[39] None of these fits its context well—and all of them are identical, in form and attitude to the manner in which the settlement was carried out, to the J-notices in Num. 32:39–42. It is eminently likely that we are dealing here with scattered sections of J's settlement report. All of these passages in Jos. 15–19 are parallel to parts of Jud. 1, some in fact being perfect doublets.[40] They are doubtless derived from it, or at least from the source of which Jud. 1 was once a part.

Mowinckel rejects Alt's view that the chapter was an independent document listing the claim of each tribe to a particular area,[41] and Noth's that it was a conglomerate of old fragments of tradition.[42] It does not have the accidental character of a conglomerate—its author worked to a plan which may still be detected—nor the character of a list. It opens with a narrative consecutive imperfect, and so is a fragment[43] of a narrative which is historical (or intended as such). What is now the beginning of the chapter must have been preceded by some report of how the Israelites had come to where Jud. 1:1 assumed them to be. There had most likely been a narrative of the crossing of the Jordan and the taking of Jericho—and if this were the case, there would have been a material and chronological link with the earlier narratives preserved in part in Jos. 2. It is not historical in the precise sense of that term—the author had clearly no information about the actual history of the conquest. The account is organized in a south-north sequence, apart from the fact that it had to start in central Palestine because of the author's assumption about the position of the Israelites at the beginning of their settlement. That accommodation is sufficient proof that the chapter *was* intended as a historical account of the settlement. The chapter's present context shows that the Deuteronomist found some connection between its contents and the calamities of the period of the Judges—but it does not rest happily in this context, for it views the settlement not from a critical negative point of view but from a positive one. The author certainly wants to communicate just to what extent it was possible in that period for the tribes to occupy the land—but he is still quite free from the later legendary conception of a complete and decisive conquest.

It was written later than Solomon—it assumes the post-Davidic 12-tribe system. Certainly there is no mention of Reuben and Gad—but that only confirms Mowinckel's working hypothesis that Jud. 1 derives from J, who had dealt with their settlement in Num. 32:39–42(!). Issachar too is unmentioned—but its boundaries (see too P's problems with that tribe in Jos. 19:17–22) were very fluid.[44] There is nothing in Jud. 1 which conflicts with the hypothesis that it is a part of J's account of the settlement. In itself it is incomplete, assuming an earlier account of the conquest of Transjordan which is provided in Num. 32. If this connection with the relevant verses in that chapter is correct, then we are dealing in Jud. 1 with the original J, and not with any of the later expansions denoted by the 'E' of the literary critics. Such developments are often ideologically on the way to the view of history and the theology of the Deuteronomist, and have nothing in common with the archaic and more historical view of Jud. 1.

The chapter on the conquest history of the Deuteronomistic historical work is the shortest and least polemical in the book. Mowinckel is in wide agreement with Noth over both the contributions of the Deuteronomist and the basically aetiological nature[45] of the material—and of course that the Deuteronomist had most of the material available to him as a collection. Mowinckel's main difference is his added assumption that since this collection is structured like Jud. 1, it must be an expanded form of J, i.e. J^v. His next thesis is that the Deuteronomistic saga also contained a report of the division of the land—and that for this too certain anecdotes from J had been used. The passages 17:14–18;[46] 18:2–10;[47] 19:49–50 (and also the somewhat different 14:6–15) appear Deuteronomistic, and do not fit their present context well. This context the earlier critics ascribed to P—and Noth showed belonged neither to the Deuteronomist's work nor to his source. Jos. 14:6–15 treats the same subject as 15:13–19 (=Jud. 1:12–15, 20) and is a later development of it; it is connected with 11:21–23[48] and breaks the connection between 14:5 and 15:1; and in its assumption that Joshua carried out the division of the land in the camp at Gilgal it fits the situation in Jos. 2–11 very well. Indeed the reference to the camp in 18:9 is probably to the same place. Furthermore the conception of division of the land by a commission of tribal representatives rather than by Joshua—referred to in 19:49–50 as well as 18:2ff.—is quite different from that in the rest of Jos. 14–19. The most natural conclusion is that where Jos. 13–21 now stand there once stood a different Deuteronomistic account of the division of the land by the tribes—and so too in his source. This will have had similar characteristics to the pre-Deuteronomistic story of the conquest—including additions from J. There is then every likelihood that it is from this source that Jos. 17:14–18 derives. The original history of the conquest in Jos. 2–11; 24 has in common with Jud. 1(J) that it deals only with the west of the Jordan. One must postulate an earlier chapter of this conquest history—and that is to be found in Num. 32 whose presuppositions are those of the conquest history. If a link with Num. 32 can be established, then Noth's denial that the Deuteronomist's source was connected with a Pentateuch source is called in question.

The third main chapter of the book deals with the conquest of the land in P. Mowinckel feels it is methodologically appropriate to open with the question whether a conquest history ought to be expected of P.[49] But even before he deals with this question, he makes clear that there is no reason to assign the insertion of P-passages into the history of Joshua to the same redactor(s) as was(were) responsible for the creation of our Pentateuch—

he had clearly combined P with Deuteronomy to form a law-book of Moses stretched over a historical frame. If P-passages had been combined with the rest of Joshua then this would have taken place after the formation of the Pentateuch and using it as a model. Furthermore, if P did write a history of the conquest, then we may assume from the rest of his work that it was very short and in summary form, included lists of names and numbers, and contained much learned information. Noth agrees that the tradition P follows and the plan on which it is constructed derive ultimately from J. Of course his interests were not historical like J's. But he began with institutions laid down at the creation of the world—how could he have failed to report the crowning of the whole story, the realization of the revealed institutions on the soil of the promised land?

Noth accepts as part of the original P, Num. 27:12–23 and also 13:2; 20:12b; and 22:1—these show that P *did* report the settlement.[50] Mowinckel finds elements of P in Num. 32, and concludes that since there is evidence that P is represented in the narrative sections of the end of the book of Numbers, there is no good reason to deny to it 33:50–34:29—and the same is true of 35:9–15.[51] He then restates the old view that there are traces of P in Jos. 2–12: the precise date in 4:19; the mention of the first passover in Canaan in 5:10–12; and the part of the narrative in 9 which talks of the 'leaders of the congregation'—i.e. vv. 15b–21. He also ascribes to P the whole of 12—certainly P had not written a *history* of the conquest, but he had confirmed the fact of the conquest and of its completeness in a list.[52]

Next he offers a critique of Alt's and Noth's studies on Jos. 13–19. Much of this is repeated from his already-reviewed earlier work on the subject[53]—but it is here set in a wider context. 19:51a is clearly the conclusion of the whole of 14–19. However the situation that verse envisages is expressly that of 18:1—since 18:2–9 are not an original part of these chapters it may be concluded that 18:1 was originally the introduction to the whole complex and that its transposition to its present place occurred during the combination of these chapters with the Deuteronomistic report (which had described a two-stage division). Noth's replies to his earlier criticisms about the lists[54] fail to justify his method: source-separation cannot be applied successfully to a list; and his literary-critical attempt to turn a boundary description into a pure list of names is so questionable an operation that it must be renounced. And as for the solution of tribal disputes—Jud. 12:1–6 shows instructively that Ephraim just fought it out with Gilead!

Mowinckel now examines his assumption that Jos. 13–19 is a connected literary complex. Noth limits the complex to 14–19, citing the introduction and conclusion in 14:1, 4a, 5 and 19:49a. But 19:49a cannot be separated from the rest of 49–50—the real conclusion is v. 51a; and while the opening verses of chapter 14 are certainly an introduction, it is not necessarily to the whole complex.[55] However the complex is not restricted to these six chapters. There can be no stylistic or literary doubt that in its present form Jos. 21:1–42 was written by the same author as 14–19.[56] Then the report of the post-conquest division in 14–19; 21 assumes in its final chapter on the Levitical cities an earlier settlement in Transjordan—and it is likely that this complex opened by describing that. There is nothing to prevent us seeing 13:15–32 as this account—and it in its turn may be judged the literary continuation of chapter 12. There is narrative in this complex—and sufficient for the whole to be termed narrative.

Mowinckel repeats the arguments of his previous study that the atmosphere of the whole narrative is post-exilic and even Jewish. Here he adds a further indication of anti-Samaritan tendency. P's placing the assembly of the whole congregation of Israel at Shiloh will have been based on the old stories in 1 Samuel that in early days there was a temple of Yahweh there; however even as late as the Deuteronomist's history the memory was preserved that in the settlement period the amphictyonic centre was Shechem—P's alteration will have been the result not of historical-critical research, but of religious prejudice.

Mowinckel summarizes his argument thus: If it is certain that P did have an account of the conquest and its logical conclusion the land-division, then the conclusion seems unavoidable that the earlier literary critics were correct that we find this in Jos. 12–19; 21. If Jos. 12 is ascribed to P, then 13–19 must be too. If P is admitted to have offered an account in Num. 32 of the taking of Transjordan, and if Jos. 13:15–32 refers back to this and expands it according to principles we observe also in 14–19, then that is proof that in 13–19 we have a section of P's work. The construction of 21 is typical of P—it cannot be doubted that 21:1–42 refers to Num. 35:1–8 and is conceived as the execution of what is ordered there (and that 17:2–6 repeats what was already written in the P-passage Num. 26:28–34).

Mowinckel's general results from this monograph are that insofar as J, J^v, and P all deal with Israel's history from creation to settlement and together have contributed all the material about Israel's prehistory and the history of her settlement now found in the Pentateuch and the book of Joshua, the term 'Hexateuch' is a legitimate critical term—however, as an actual entity consisting of the Pentateuch and the book of Joshua in their present form, a 'Hexateuch' never existed. Our Pentateuch was produced by the introduction of the law-book from the beginning of the Deuteronomistic History into the already completed combination of J^v and P—as a consequence, those parts of J and P which did deal with Joshua and the settlement were worked into the corresponding part of the historical work. A 'Tetrateuch' consisting of the books Genesis to Numbers never existed.

C. Mowinckel and Noth

It was suggested above at the end of our first chapter that it was one of the weaknesses of Noth's argument that he could point to so little evidence of J's handling of the settlement theme—and it was noted that Mowinckel offered a thoroughgoing critique of Noth's literary conclusions. But—at least in the case of Num. 32—what a muddled critique! There are many small slips in these later works of Mowinckel—but the intention of the author is usually plain enough. That can hardly be said for his handling of this chapter. In *Pentateuch Quellenfrage*, the situation is reasonably clear. He renounces earlier attempts, including Noth's and his own, to divide the chapter into sources—with two exceptions it is a unity: some possibly Deuteronomizing additions (influence, that is, from the Deuteronomistic story in Joshua); and the final four verses, three of which belong to J while one forges an editorial link. The main part of the chapter is a learned aetiology of the presence in Transjordan of a two-and-a-half tribe Israelite minority. It is just possible that this aetiology has replaced J notes on Reuben and Gad similar to those on Machir in vv. 39–42—and that remnants of these can be detected in vv. 1, 4–5, 34–38. In *Tetrateuch-Pentateuch-Hexateuch*, the same point is made in the section 'J in Num. 32' (pp. 10–12)—but with two changes: there is no mention of the suppression of J-notes; but in a footnote (n. 5) Rudolph's attribution to J of vv. 2*, 4–6, 16a, 17, 20–23, 25–27, 33a*, 34–39, 41–42 is welcomed.[57] It would appear that these two approaches to J in the chapter exclude each other—and certainly in this book all Mowinckel's subsequent references to Num. 32 in connection with J make it clear that he is dealing only with vv. 39–42.[58] Yet it is to these verses he attributes mention of the settlement of Reuben and Gad (p. 24) although mention of these tribes in J in Num. 32 implies Mowinckel's earlier view of that chapter. Mowinckel's fumbling over this chapter may not be unrelated to his failure to take account of the most obvious feature of the whole chapter as we encounter it: its character may change at v. 39—but in another way it does so quite as clearly at v. 33. Verses 1–32 are only about Gad and Reuben—it is quite misleading to describe the chapter as a whole as an aetiology of the two-and-a-half Transjordanian tribes. On the other side, the mention of Manassite holdings in vv. 39–42 comes as no sudden surprise: it is prepared for by the new heading in v. 33 and the detailing of Gadite and Reubenite holdings in the following verses.

Mowinckel's generalizations about Jud. 1 give rise to similar disquiet. It is doubtful whether much of his evaluation of the chapter is based on accurate description. He stresses that its author does not enumerate but narrate.[59] Should he not, however, be said to do first one and then the other?[60] Even his later evaluation that the chapter is a review of the conquest's results prefaced by anecdotes about its start is somewhat misleading. He appears—in company with many scholars—to hold the opinion that in Jud. 1 we have an account of the Israelite conquest parallel to but less legendary than that found in the first half of the book of Joshua. It may very well be that Jud. 1 is in some respects a superior source to the book of Joshua for the modern historian who wishes to reconstruct a picture of Israel's settlement—but that is quite a different judgment from the one just quoted, and seems to have no logical connection with it.[61]

If it is not assumed that it is *Israel's* settlement which is here described, then it may be noticed that all the anecdotes which preface the chapter are about Judah[62] (and Simeon)—with the exception of the taking of Bethel by the house of Joseph. Furthermore, to link vv. 27–29 with the anecdote about Bethel as the material about the centre of the country,[63] as opposed to vv. 30ff. about the north is to do violence to the shape of the material. Finally the opening idea of 'going up' denotes military attack (as often), and not geographical ascent. In short, the arrangement of the chapter is not geographical but tribal. Judah's primacy is asserted as early as the second verse; and more than half the chapter is concerned with her. Even the note on the house of Joseph cannot deflect our attention from the emphasis of the chapter on the success of Judah and the failure of the rest of the tribes.[64] And since this is so, it is appropriate to judge the chapter both positive and negative in outlook.

The very fact that Mowinckel opens his chapter on P's history of the conquest with the observation that the P we may find in the book of Joshua may not be quite the same as the P of the Pentateuch—just a source, and not the basic plan of the whole work as well[65]—leads one to suspect, by its very sophistication, that the chapter will be a defence of a position rather than a cumulative argument towards one. Since the literary situation is different, the argument that we may *expect* of P a conquest-story must carry even more of the weight of the whole discussion than did the parallel argument in the case of J. Accordingly Mowinckel backs this argument with three reasons: (1) if P did not deal with the conquest, we would be faced with an unaccountable break with the shape of the tradition as shown in J; (2) without its *natural* conclusion, relating how everything proper had been done, P would be but a torso; and (3) sections at the end of the book of Numbers generally assigned to P are in fact the beginning of a conquest narrative.

Whether or not one agrees with Mowinckel on such issues, we must be grateful to him for refocusing our attention on some of the main problems of Joshua and Pentateuch. Like von Rad, it is 'tradition' that appears to occupy the centre of Mowinckel's interest. We have seen that he does not accept Engnell's estimate of his own method as being 'consistently traditio-historical'. But this 'slogan' is a fair estimate of Mowinckel's method and interest. The picture he offers of J's use of his sources, of the development of J evidenced in J^v, of P's general adherence to the plan of J and J^v—all this is ample evidence of what he means by a 'genetic' approach to the development of tradition.

Unbiassed literary appreciation may be a chimera. It is possible that Noth's appeal to the literary situation first and foremost is somewhat one-sided. But it is only accurate description of the given documents (however arrived at) that can save us from some of the unsupported assertions—and even distortions—offered by von Rad and Mowinckel on the basis of their reliance on the fidelity of tradition and constancy of form. Such description it will be the business of the second part of this thesis to attempt. But first—some account of other scholarly contributions to Joshua and the Pentateuch since 1938.

NOTES

1. In *Zur Frage* . . . (1946), p. 38, nn. 24–25, he notes that he already had the intention of publishing a critique of the views of Alt and Noth, in particular those that affect our understanding of J and Jud. 1.
2. By contrast, his *Erwägungen* (also published in 1964) does cite Noth's *HPT*, but not *Josua*[2].
3. He published two appreciations of Wellhausen on the occasion of his death in 1918, in *Norsk Kirkeblad* and *For Kirke og Kultur*. In 1923, he reviewed Eissfeldt's *Hexateuch-Synopse* for the *Norsk Teologisk Tidsskrift*. Some further impression of his attitude to contemporary Pentateuchal criticism can be gained from his important study *Le Décalogue* (1927), which was preceded in 1926 by his paper 'L'Origine du Décalogue'. Clearer evidence can be found in his contributions to the first volume (in 1929) of *Det Gamle Testamente*, a translation into Norwegian of the Pentateuch with brief introduction and commentary. The account there offered, of the combined JE worked into the Deuteronomic History with the Priestly Work later added to the whole, confirms our placing Mowinckel firmly in the Wellhausen tradition at this stage in his career. In the same period he made some observations about the relationship of J and E in 'Der Ursprung der Bileamsage'. Probing the remoter origins of Israel's traditions, he asked in 1935 'Hat es ein israelitisches Nationalepos gegeben?'. His 1937 monograph on the primeval history divided between J and E what is ascribed by most scholars to J alone—E, he claims, must occasionally be reconstructed from P, between which and J it occupies a middle position in the development of the tradition.
4. Here he probably exaggerates. The fact of oral tradition was allowed for, but it was not systematically treated.
5. This probably misrepresents Engnell—and indeed Nyberg whom Engnell is following. Cf. Engnell's essay 'Prophets and Prophetism', p. 166.
6. In his *Studien zum Hoseabuche.*
7. *op. cit.*, p. 30.
8. 'Die vermeintliche "Passahlegende" Ex. 1–15—in Bezug auf die Frage: Literarkritik und Traditionskritik' (1951).
9. Not only in *ZAW* 52, pp. 161ff., but also in an additional note 'The Crossing of the Red Sea and the Paschal Legend' in *Israel* III–IV, pp. 728–737.
10. Mowinckel notes that the view cannot be dismissed *a priori* that the sources were woven together by a saga-artist working orally; but it is at least as possible that this was a literary piece of work—and the nature of the redaction of the flood-story makes this latter view more likely.
11. *Zur Frage nach dokumentarischen Quellen in Josua 13–19* (1946).
12. 'Überlieferungsgeschichtliches zur zweiten Hälfte des Josuabuches' (1950).

13. Cf. above pp. 3, 4 and n. 10.
14. 'Judas Gaue unter Josia' (1925).
15. Jos. 15:21–62; 18:21–28; 19:2–7, 41–46. On p. 7, Mowinckel appears to have unintentionally omitted the name of Benjamin.
16. Cf. above n. 12.
17. As described above, pp. 19–20.
18. The debate between Noth and Mowinckel on this point closely resembles that between Noth and von Rad mentioned above, p. 29.
19. Noth concludes this study with a short discussion of Jos. 21 prompted by Albright's essay in the Ginzberg volume, 'The List of the Levitic Cities' (1945). Noth observes that any interpretation of this list must start from the consideration that Hebron and Shechem (which are later insertions) are the only cities representing the heartlands of Judah and Ephraim—the original list had had these two large geographical gaps.
20. The two posthumous publications, *Kanaan for Israel* and *Israels opphav og eldste historie*—both of 1967, need not concern us here: they presuppose the literary-critical and traditio-historical results of the earlier three which *are* of more relevance to our discussion.
21. 'Israelite Historiography' (1963).
22. *Die Anfänge der israelitischen Geschichtsschreibung* (1942), revised and expanded in *Geschichtsschreibung in Israel* (1952).
23. *Quellenfrage* (1964).
24. Noting that in practice this means Genesis-Numbers.
25. *Untersuchungen zum Hexateuchproblem* (1924).
26. His was the larger share in *Der Elohist als Erzähler* (1933).
27. *Composition*[3], pp. 336ff. Mowinckel observes that for the patriarchal period P adds only Gen. 17; 23 to J's framework.
28. He remarks that Wellhausen had introduced his analysis of the Joseph-story thus: 'It may be assumed that here as elsewhere this work' (i.e. JE) 'is composed of J and E; our earlier results urge this assumption and would be shaken were it not demonstrable.' (*Composition*[3], p. 52).
29. Here he concedes the failure of his own attempt in *The Two Sources* . . . (1937)—cf. above n. 3.
30. At this point Mowinckel adheres to the results of his earlier study—cf. again n. 3: 'Der Ursprung der Bileamsage'.
31. *Erwägungen*, pp. 102–104.
32. On p. 104(l.5), v. 34 is clearly a mistake for v. 39.
33. Perhaps originally located after Jos. 11.
34. It is nothing short of a miracle (p. 111) that, given this development of the tradition, J's early review in Jud. 1 was actually preserved.
35. *T-P-H* (1964).
36. In *Gamla Testamentet* (1945).
37. Rather inconsequentially, the title of the first section of this chapter is 'J in *Ex*-Num has as its goal . . .'.
38. More precisely vv. 39, 41, 42—v. 40 is redactional (see above p. 26).
39. He mentions (p. 15) 15:13–19; 15:63; 16:10; 17:12–13; 17:14–18; 19:47. In the parallel discussion in *Quellenfrage*, p. 107, he adds 13:13 but does not include 17:12.
40. That of course is not true of 13:13 and may be the reason for its non-mention (cf. above n. 39). However, it is equally untrue of 17:14–18.
41. *KS* I, pp. 193ff.
42. *UGS*, p. 9.
43. This does not follow at all—Jonah, Ruth and Esther all open in a similar way.
44. Another post-Solomonic feature, for Mowinckel, is the mention several times

of a tribe putting the Canaanites to forced labour.

45. Indeed this study concludes (pp. 78–86) with an excursus on aetiological thought.
46. So p. 44—but on p. 15 (see above n. 39) 17:14–18 was listed with the J-notes.
47. In the argument that follows he in fact restricts his attention to vv. 2–9.
48. Mowinckel suggests that 14:7, 10 make more precise the detail in 11:18. While 13:1, 7–8a do not fit their present context they do agree with those chronological details, and so are probably the opening of D's land-division account.
49. He notes that Wellhausen had originally denied Jos. 13–21 to P *because* he found no trace in the preceding chapters of a conquest history of P. It was the arguments of Graf, Kuenen and others which later induced him to give up this approach.
50. Mowinckel quotes (p. 55) Noth's argument that the Sinai pericope was P's main interest—but not the complementary one, that P was concerned to conclude with the history of Moses.
51. After all the mistakes in his own work it is amusing to find Mowinckel (p. 57) blaming Noth for an *Inkonsequenz* over these verses. Certainly Noth (*UGS*, pp. 192ff., and especially p. 195) quotes with approval the accepted point of view that 35:(1–8) 16–34; 36:1–13 is a later addition to P. But it is quite as clear (to this reader at least) that this approval does not involve Noth in ascribing 35:9–15 to P—it is rather only *these* verses whose ascription to P requires discussion.
52. The MT with its 31 names is overloaded—30 is a number which traditionally denotes completeness (p. 60).
53. See above pp. 20–22.
54. See above pp. 22–23.
55. Mowinckel states that P has many such examples of introductory and concluding formulae for individual sub-sections.
56. This against Noth who considered it a later supplement. However Noth is correct that 19:51b–20:9 is a later insertion into its present context.
57. *Der 'Elohist'*, p. 134.
58. *T-P-H*, pp. 16, 24, 30, 32.
59. *op. cit.*, p. 19.
60. Narration mainly in the first part of the chapter, and enumeration of results (or their lack) in the second.
61. This point is made more fully in my own discussion of Jud. 1: *VT* 25, p. 285.
62. In the widest sense of that name.
63. As in *T-P-H*, p. 24 and (at least by implication) p. 26.
64. Smend, in his paper 'Gehörte Judah zum vorstaatlichen Israel?', suggested that some passages in Judges may have been re-edited to Judah's advantage.
65. *T-P-H*, p. 53.

CHAPTER III

CONTINUING DEBATE

A. Topographical Studies

Alt's and Noth's conviction that in their historico-geographical deductions from the text of the book of Joshua they were able to penetrate behind the book's literary 'sources' or 'strata' to its actual material—its 'sources' in the commoner historical use of that term—has also been found very fruitful. This has perhaps been especially true of their suggestion that the majority of an administrative list of the state of Judah can be extricated from the town-list in Jos. 15:21–62. This is divided into eleven sections, at least in the fuller and preferable text of the LXX.[1] In fact Noth considered there are twelve sections—treating v. 45 as the stump of a section, distinct from the later supplement in vv. 46–47. By linking that verse with the Danite list in 19:41–46,[2] vv. 61–62 with the first Benjaminite list in 18:21–24 and v. 60 with the second in 18:25–28[3]—in each case the basis for the linkage is one name common to both parts—he claimed to have reconstructed a division of Judah dating from the first military successes of Josiah.

In the first attempted refinement of this, Cross and Wright[4] address themselves to the persistence of certain problems in this scheme.

> The linking of 18:21–24 with 15:61–62 they find geographical nonsense.[5] And, while they do offer detailed arguments against linking 19:41–46 with either 15:33–36 or 15:45–47, they stress that the tribal boundary system leaves a gap for Dan[6] and so it is improper to link it with a Judahite area.

Their preferred solution is to consider the Benjaminite towns of 18:21–28 as a whole the twelfth Judahite district. The small part of Ephraim so included represents not the annexation of Josiah, which was much more extensive, but that of Abijah of Judah from Jeroboam—held at least till the time of Jehoshaphat, to whose reign various details point as the date for this form of the division.[7]

Kallai's quite distinct approach to the same problems was the next to appear.[8] He assented to the differentiation between the boundary system and the town lists. The probable origin of the former was David's census; and he stresses that its geographical and chronological framework is shared by both the list of still unconquered areas in Jud. 1 and the list of Levitical cities (especially the form found in 1 Chr. 6 with its exclusion of Dan—leaving Judah, Benjamin and Ephraim to meet without remainder).[9] The town lists are separate documents, each describing its own tribe, and not necessarily at a common date. The appropriate method for studying these is to judge each 'document' as it is preserved, not to establish an original core by weeding out later additions. He deduces that the Judahite list, while it may have originated under Jehoshaphat, clearly reflects the reign of Hezekiah; that Dan's is based on the second district of Solomon; and that Benjamin's (18:21–28 has lost one of its original three units[10]—the exception which proves Kallai's rule of fidelity to the text as transmitted!?), which he agrees is marked by northernly expansion, reflects the conquest of Abijah.[11] Cross and Wright were wrong to use this evidence in their discussion of the Judahite list—not all the conquests of Abijah remained in Judah's hands as long as Jehoshaphat.

Kallai's assurance that he is dealing with documents, coupled with his basic premiss about the unified boundary system, leads him to one statement of principle which again suggests his respect for the received text is only relative. While discussing Dan, he argues that the area of its town list is fully covered by the allotments to Judah and Ephraim. To understand that there is in fact no 'Danite gap' one has to remember that a town stands for its whole territory, and so the limits of each must be ascertained. The El-Amarna tablets show that in their period Gezer, which Israel's system of boundaries assigns to Ephraim, included both Ajalon and Zoreah. And so Ephraimite territory filled the area west of Benjamin and north of Judah.[12] With the conquest of this area by the Pharaoh who then presented it to Solomon, all this area became in fact Israelite. To this Kallai adds in a footnote that boundary systems cannot be deduced for Simeon and Dan by literary methods based on the wording of verses like Jos. 19:8 and 46—the criterion for a town-list unaccompanied by parallel boundary-list is that the territory described is included in the area of other tribes, and this holds for these two.

Kallai does emphasize his broad agreement that the extent and internal division of the town lists do reflect political situations and as such let us have a glimpse of what an administrative list of the whole kingdom would have looked like. However it is the tribal situation which is the main factor in these town lists—they were not cut up, but were drawn up to show the holdings of the particular tribe in a given political situation.[13]

Kallai subsequently published a much fuller account of his researches into Israel's historical geography.[14] This the present writer can claim only to have sampled widely, and read in detail only on selected points. It appears to represent a furthering of the research just reviewed rather than an advance on it. In particular it confirms our impression of his confidence that he is dealing in the main with documents of the period of the First Temple which have been little altered by those who are termed the 'biblical editors' without further discrimination.

At the conclusion of a recent article[15] he offers a cautious restatement of this position. The United Monarchy is presented as the matrix of many of the Bible's geographical concepts. 'This conclusion is regardless of whether the period served only as a primary pattern, which was further developed at a later stage. This is conceivable at a time when the need was felt to lean on this period of greatness and to base on it the historical tenets coupled with the expressions of legitimization required for the historiosophical view that permeates Israel's world of ideas. Periods of great crisis in the history of the Kingdom of Judah may have prompted such spiritual and scribal activity, and the material may have been re-edited later again.'

Aharoni's study of Judah's province list falls next to be considered.[16] He approves of some of the advances made by Cross and Wright, and also Kallai, on Alt's profound proposals, but finds that the relation between the area of the provinces and the boundary of Judah at different times has not been satisfactorily solved. Kallai's conclusion that the lists of Judah and Benjamin are of different origins eliminates some difficulties but bypasses the main problem: the list of Judah is south of Jerusalem and so can never be identical with the territory of the Judahite kingdom; also Kallai offers no alternative purpose for the town lists, of which Jos. 15 enumerates eleven in Judah. Turning his attention to the Benjaminite towns, he notes that Cross and Wright's view that the two groups are separated by the watershed is not quite accurate—what he finds significant is that while the towns of the second group were in most periods in the Kingdom of Judah those in the first were regularly in Israel. Accordingly it is the second group only which is the missing twelfth district of Judah. Following an argument of Alt that among the sources of Jos. 19 were towns lists for the northern tribes, Aharoni goes on to argue that these and the first Benjaminite group reflect the administrative division of the northern kingdom[17]—only in that framework was it logical to unite Bethel and Jericho in one district![18] This makes it likely that it was within Benjamin that most of the border conflicts between Judah and Israel took place; and also helps to explain the double mention of Beth-arabah—a border city between the two states.

Aharoni's contribution to the study of Israel's historical geography is also available in much more detailed form in a study translated into English as *The Land of the Bible.*[19] Like Kallai, Aharoni is confident that he is dealing with documents; and like him too he is quite unspecific about the biblical editors. He marshalls attractively the 'documents' gleaned from the book of Joshua and elsewhere to illustrate Israel's history and political geography in five periods from the Canaanite till the latter days of the Judean Kingdom. Many of his detailed arguments, and his synthesis as a whole, are very suggestive. But perhaps one should have more scruples over the use of 'the land which remains' (Jos. 13:2–6) and the 'list' of unconquered cities in Jud. 1 to illustrate the period of conquest and settlement. This material in Jud. 1:21, 27–35 serves as a pillar for another case: coupled with the further assertion that the tribal framework west of the Jordan lacks not only territories for Issachar, Dan and Simeon but also for Judah—its frontiers are a simple amalgam of the relevant portions of the frontiers of the promised land (as in Num. 34) together with the southern border of Benjamin—he argues that the boundary list in Joshua represents basically the relationships of a six-tribe northern Israelite covenant (the same six tribes as are reflected in the basis of the material in Jud. 1 already referred to[20]). Arguments of this order either assume (without stating) or else ignore (perhaps without realizing) important literary considerations.

This is not the occasion for a thorough review of Aharoni's work in this field. However two further details of his conclusions may be mentioned to illustrate this point further. He follows his account of the northern covenant by hailing David as the bringer of the new unity which remained an ideal in later times, not just because of the greatness and extent of the state then achieved under him but also because the aims of his political and religious settlement were fostered in the milieu of the Jerusalem Temple (many of whose institutions and traditions he shaped even if he did not build the building). He claims that David's administrative division was traditionalist and tribalist in nature—and by that he appears to mean that David employed a traditional (i.e. commonly used) 12-fold system which adhered as closely as possible to existing tribal patterns—and argues that this division is illustrated by the account of his census and by the city lists for Simeon and Dan. Two resultant problems may be noted:

(1) He finds evidence for the Simeonite list only in 19:2–6—the second and shorter Simeonite 'district' in 19:7 he rejects as a later expansion of the text.

(2) The account in 2 Sam. 24 of David's census knows of Dan in the north. If this is accurate, and if the (ancient!) tradition in Jud. 1 about the inability of Dan to secure its holding in the centre of the country is also accurate, then in what sense does the list of cities recorded in Jos. 19:41–46 reflect either ancient tribal or Danite realities?

The second of his conclusions to be discussed has implications related to the first of these points. His rationale for the brief two-town list in 15:60 is that Kiriath-jearim and Rabbah (=the El-Amarna Rubute=the familiar Beth-Shemesh) dominated the strategic main road from the coast to Jerusalem and were thus sufficiently important to constitute a distinct entity. His case so far is not unattractive. However it continues as follows: To the hypothesis that Rabbah/Rubute is Beth-Shemesh (a view that he has since changed[21]) he adds the claim that Zorah and Eshtaol, of the first Shephelah district in 15:33, must have originally belonged to this list represented in 15:60 whose territory included that part of Dan in Judean hands. To render this plausible he has to make two assumptions about the development of Jos. 15:21–62. The first follows from his observation 'that in geographical descriptions the hill country is always mentioned before the Shephelah'[22]—our list had accordingly once been structured this way. The second appears to harmonize rather ill with the first: that the geographical designations (and also presumably the concluding totals although he does not mention these) were not an original part of the text. These allow him to reconstruct his 'original': 'Kiriathbaal, Rabbah, Eshtaol, Zorah/Ashnah, Zanoah, etc.'.[23] Respect for the 'realities' which *must* be involved is a formidable tool for the solution of literary problems!

Schunck's study of the origins and history of the tribe of Benjamin[24] is an attractive demonstration—although not designed as such—of how readily some of Aharoni's arguments can be 'stood on their heads'.[25] He is convinced up to a point that Mowinckel, followed by Kallai, was right to doubt the view of Alt and Noth that a single ancient tradition lies behind the tribal system in Jos. 13–19. But that our present text is based on several different sources or documents is still better than the counter view of Mowinckel and Kallai. He claims that one of these border descriptions is to be assigned with certainty to the time of David—15:2–12a. A supplementary list was added in the time of Rehoboam—16:1–3, which is closely related to 15:2–12a, and not originally a description of Joseph's southern boundary. Much more likely is it that it was a replacement for the line described in 15:5b–11. Schunck's attendant claim is that the whole of Benjamin was included in the kingdom of Judah. However he is insistent that this may not be clarified by appeal to the border descriptions in Jos. 18—these are in fact a combination of 15:2–12a and 16:1–3 that pays attention to the Danite list in 19:40ff! So much for his alternative account of the tribal border system.[26] His account of the ancient (!) material in Jud. 1 opens with the stylistic observation that mention of Benjamin and Dan obtrudes somewhat, in that both tribes are referred to as *bny-*, and not just with their simple names. Behind this chapter he accordingly assumes the traditions of a six-tribe unit: Judah, Manasseh, Ephraim, Zebulun, Asher and Naphtali—the descriptions of whose situations are similar in style. Aharoni's six-tribe 'covenant' had included Benjamin, not Judah.

A pair of detailed studies of just one of these problems we have reviewed—the Danite list of Jos. 19:40ff.—provide a further example of the widely different results achieved in this area of study. Mazar[27] argues that this list is made up of four districts, the first two[28] representing the second of Solomon's administrative districts, according to 1 Kings 4, and the second two reflecting an expansion which itself cannot be later than the death of Solomon.[29] Strange,[30] on the other hand, argues that control of Ekron and the immediate coastal strip implies a stricter form of control than either Judah or Israel in their status as separate kingdoms could ever have enforced, and that there is no evidence that Solomon ever controlled it. Only after the exhaustion of Philistia in her several revolts against Assyria is such control conceivable. It had been in the interest of Assyria's Egyptian policy to allow her vassal Judah under Josiah to expand somewhat westwards—this had suited Josiah who required access to the sea before he could begin to realize his ambition of succeeding to the glories of Solomon's commercial empire.[31]

The next of these studies we must mention is Simons' magnum opus on the OT's geographical texts,[32] limiting our attention to his account of the texts in the second half of the book of Joshua.

In his introduction to the problems of the descriptions of the territories of the Transjordanian tribes he offers some general comments which are indicative of his views about and approach to the whole matter in hand. He detects much amplification in the texts, and the possibility that originally different conceptions have been smoothed out. Yet his final impression is of greater consistency in the texts than is generally assumed, whether this is original or in fact the result of later levelling. He notes that all attempts to prove manipulations of the text and lay bare the main outlines of the 'real' course of events have hitherto been very unsatisfactory. And so his guiding principle of interpretation is to limit the number and size of emendations of the MT to the indispensable minimum.

However Simons does believe that some evidence of earlier editorial intentions has been preserved in Jos. 13–14: 13:1, 7 were originally the introduction to the description of the Cisjordanian territories in 14–19—this is shown both by the abrupt beginning of the Transjordanian descriptions (with *'mw* in 13:8) and by 14:1–5 which is a secondary introduction necessitated merely by the insertion of 13:8ff. Whatever one's critical conclusion about 13:8, v. 9 starts a new description of the collective territorial claims of these tribes.[33]

Simons' book lives up to its promise of a sober approach to the text.[34] It provides a welcome change from divisions of quite readable texts on the basis of none too secure theories about sources and developments. Furthermore, not only does Simons respect the text in a formal way—he also reads what it actually says with sensitivity. And yet two questions should be borne in mind when assessing his results: (1) Do some of his few emendations remove any evidence of strands? (2) Does his refusal to probe more closely the editorial strata within the second half of Joshua, despite his awareness that they exist, result in a carelessness as to just whose editorial point of view he is expounding in this very fair presentation?

Finally Bächli has offered some interesting observations on the literary transition from source-lists to the narrative descriptions in Jos. 13–19.[35] He suggests that the several verbs of motion and change of location used in the territorial descriptions and the kind of features cited for orientation are best explained by the hypothesis that the descriptions are those that would have been produced by a commission traversing the land on foot. Record of such a commission is preserved in Jos. 18:1–10 and this fact enables deductions about the literary relationship between that narrative and the detailed lists. Bächli adds that the existence of such commissions is vouched for by the census story in 2 Sam. 24.

If any concluding comment to this section of our introduction is required, it must be that the historical geographer and topographer should not consider that he has free access to readily dated and authenticated documentary material in the book of Joshua. The insights of Alt and Noth in this area of study have been acclaimed and appropriated by many who have not shared their sensitivity to the literary and other related problems of the texts to which they in turn seek to appeal.

B. Literary Studies

(1) *Articles and Monographs*

The study which makes all such accounts of the literature appear inadequate is Jenni's masterly article of 1961/2 on the previous two decades of research on the books Joshua to Kings.[36] Of the studies on the town lists of Judah reviewed above and available then he appears to have been most in sympathy with Aharoni. Part of the function of this present chapter is to go some way to bringing Jenni's survey up to date.

Eissfeldt offered a new scrutiny of his own thesis in the light of the studies of Noth and their growing acceptance, in his article on Deuteronomy and the Hexateuch published in 1966.[37] In fact it is less of a new scrutiny than a restatement of the old Hexateuchal source-critical thesis which he felt Noth's approach had not really endangered. He reaffirmed that the pre-Deuteronomistic material in Joshua required analysis into parallel strands—and that while two such sufficed in chapters 8–11 three were required in the earlier part of the book. The fact that this analysis is so similar to that demanded by the earlier material in Genesis to Numbers, when taken with the observation that Joshua recounts what is expected and promised throughout the Pentateuch, confirms that the earlier strata in Joshua are the continuation of those in the Pentateuch. Furthermore the content and language of much of the material in the second half of Joshua is clearly that of the Pentateuchal P. As for the book of Deuteronomy too, the older view is still preferable that in 1:1–4:40 and 4:44–11:32 we encounter the introductions to once separate editions of the Deuteronomic law, editions which were in due time inserted into the framework of the pre-Deuteronomic proto-Hexateuch.

That the first few chapters of Joshua do exhibit a much more complex structure than those that follow has been amply confirmed in a series of studies which have paid close attention to their literary and traditio-historical problems, although without necessarily having recourse to the kind of source-criticism which Noth rejected. The keenest problems of all are posed by Jos. 3–4. The special studies by Möhlenbrink,[38] Kraus,[39] Dus,[40] Maier,[41] Vogt,[42] Schmid,[43] Soggin[44] and others are fully documented and fairly discussed in that of Langlamet,[45] deemed the most thorough to date (in 1971) by de Vaux who offers this summary:[46] 'He has divided the early materials and the editorial elements[47] in Jos. 3–4 into nine subdivisions: (1) an Israelitic version, without the figure of Joshua, of the aetiology of the stones of Gilgal; (2) a "Shittim-Gilgal" story; (3) an "ark" story; (4) an aetiology of the stones in the Jordan; (5) a "Joshua" version of the aetiology of the Gilgal stones; (6) two Gilgal catechisms; (7) a first Deuteronomistic redaction; (8) the texts of the Deuteronomistic historian or his school; (9) brief later additions.' Langlamet's subsequent studies of Jos. 2[48] and Jos. 3–4[49] will be more usefully reviewed later in this study (in chapter VI below). In them he returns to Eissfeldt's general framework, and may be reckoned a more powerful advocate of it than the old master himself. Two further analyses, roughly contemporary with Langlamet's, offer yet more novel perspectives. Wilcoxen[50] analyzes Jos. 1–6 on the model of Pedersen's treatment of Ex. 1–15; while Wijngaards[51] detects the interplay of Shechemite and Gilgalite traditions as the main complicating feature in the narrative of Jos. 3–4. The more recent study by Porter[52] returns to and develops the cultic approach of Kraus and Soggin. He finds Langlamet's argumentation circular and echoing 'the worst excesses of the good old heyday of Pentateuchal criticism'. Wilcoxen he cites apparently with approval. Porter's own paper sketches an impressively coherent account of some of the more stubborn problems of Jos. 3–5; however one suspects he is saved by the aim and scope of his study from having to account in detail for the literary transition from the festival (which is the background to our chapters) to the inherited text. Then Otto's analysis of Jos. 1–12 (though his interest is concentrated particularly on chapters 3–6) into two largely parallel sources representing the activity of the traditional Yahwist and Deuteronomist of the Pentateuch must, like Langlamet's work occupy our attention below in chapter VI.[53] Smend's important argument[54] that Jos. 13:1a, on Joshua's advanced years, is prior to Jos. 23:1b (the reverse of Noth's position) and drafted by the first Deuteronomistic editor will be one of the pillars of our argument in chapter IV.

Since the researches of Noth and Mowinckel there has been almost no discussion of the literary relationships of the final chapters of Numbers, outside the Commentaries and Introductions to be mentioned below. Mittman has offered analyses of Num. 20:1–13; 27:12–23; and 32 in the context of his discussion of Deut. 3:18–29 on the preparation for the settlement west of the Jordan.[55] And there is now available one detailed and resolute attempt to plot the inter-relationships of the traditions in Numbers and Joshua about Israel's settlement in Transjordan. The many ramifications of Wüst's study[56] will be seen throughout the next two chapters to have stimulated many of the details of their discussion. His questions are very much my own, although our answers are radically different.

Finally, comment on Tengström's[57] and Rendtorff's[58] contemporaneous but very different accounts of the genesis of the Pentateuch/Hexateuch may best await our concluding chapter.

(2) *Commentaries*

Marsh's commentary on Numbers[59] represents a restatement of the old position on the book's final chapters: chapter 32 is seen as a mix of JEDP, while chapters 33–36 are ascribed to P with the exception of 33:50–56 which is a mixture of P, H and D.

Snaith too finds that the end of Numbers is mostly from P. His discussion of chapter 32 is interesting and helpful. He claims none of it for JE, noting that the campaigns against Sihon and Og are regarded in the earlier traditions (JE and D) as being wholly independent of the request of Gad and Reuben as reported here. He finds the involvement of P-editors at least in vv. 28–32.[60]

Sturdy's recent work[61] pays much attention to literary detail, for all its brevity. He directs our attention to the reconciliation of two different principles of land-allocation in 26:52–56, the later 33:54 offering a more coherent statement of the matter. Then he suggests that Num. 28–36 are later insertions to the P-source, following which Deuteronomy had been added to produce the Pentateuch much as we know it. Finally much of chapter 32 is from J, expanded by P.

The commentaries on the book of Joshua published since the first appearance of Noth's can also be briefly reviewed. These, almost without exception, *have* adopted his fundamental analysis. This is true of Abel,[62] whose succinct commentary is to be welcomed for its positive appreciation of the testimony of LXX^B to the text of Joshua; Hertzberg;[63] and Bright.[64] Their introductory sections are fairly brief, and only general orientation can be expected of them, not detailed comment.[65]

The scope of Gray's work is larger, being a commentary on Judges and Ruth as well as Joshua.[66] His general introduction to Joshua and Judges is basically an approving restatement of Noth's views about the Deuteronomistic History, with detailed criticism reserved only for the latter's chronological scheme. He agrees that the Deuteronomist had available to him as source-material compilations such as those in Jos. 2–11 and Jud. 3:7–12:7; and argues that such traditions and tradition-complexes were either parts of larger compilations available also to J and E or composed about the same time as J and E (and perhaps using these as a model), rather than actual sections of J and E. His introduction to Joshua emphasizes, in contradistinction to von Rad, that 'the unity of subject in the Law and Joshua is more apparent than real.'[67] While many of his answers differ from Noth's it is worth noting that it is to the same questions or kinds of question that he is addressing himself.

This is true also of the work of Soggin,[68] who is quite explicit that 'the discovery made by Martin Noth during the Second World War supplies the key for the whole interpretation of the "former prophets" of the Hebrew canon.'[69] His description of the Deuteronomistic and post-Deuteronomistic elements in Joshua is virtually indistinguishable from Noth's. However the end of his discussion of the pre-history of Jos. 1–12 is hard to understand.[70]

He mentions Noth's detection of pre-Deuteronomistic editorial links in 5:1; 6:27; 9:3–4a; 10:2, 5, 40–42; 11:1–2, 16–20; but then immediately suggests that 'the most notable attempt to locate and isolate the pre-Deuteronomic material is certainly that recently carried out by Mowinckel'. Soggin apparently endorses the latter's isolation of Jos. 2; 11:13[71] as representing the earliest detectable stratum of settlement traditions; but prefers Noth's neutral 'compiler' (*Sammler*) to Mowinckel's J as a label for its author. Now, as the passages just quoted from Joshua make clear, the efforts of Noth's compiler and Mowinckel's J do not overlap. Furthermore, as the discussion in chapter II above made clear,[72] Mowinckel expressed almost complete agreement with Noth's account of the genesis of Jos. 1–12. All he added was that Noth's compiler should be identified as J , since his account is structured like Jud. 1 (J).[73]

The recent shorter commentary by Miller and Tucker[74] stands in the same Noth-tradition. And this leaves as a significant exception the commentary by Kaufmann.[75] Kaufmann's solutions to many of the problems of the book of Joshua as literature or as history are radically different from the mainstream of scholarship almost to the point of eccentricity. He distinguishes between a 'realistic' and an 'idealistic' stratum in the book—the terms are his, but the view is shared with many thus far. His distinctiveness is in considering the idealistic the earlier of these strata and assigning it to a period before the settlement. The land-division in Joshua is part of his idealistic stratum—and so, while his critique of Alt's and Noth's attempts to derive this material from administrative (and so 'realistic') lists overlaps to a fair extent with Mowinckel's—both emphasize the discrepancies and inadequacies in the boundary system which would not be expected of administrative material—the dating of it is totally different.

(3) *Introductions*

As is perhaps hardly surprising, the familiar introductions to the literature of the Old Testament offer little advance on this situation. Broadly speaking, the two first and most basic theses of Noth with which Mowinckel too declared himself in agreement—that the distinctively Deuteronomistic redaction of Joshua marks the literary history of that book off from that of the Pentateuch and that this redaction is the principal characteristic of the books Deuteronomy to Kings as a whole—have found widespread acceptance. These are of course the least novel elements of Noth's contribution—however it is *his* statement of the situation that has become widely used.

Again in general terms, those introductions whose earlier editions had already been published before Noth's studies appeared or whose authors were already well-established when his work became known have noted but have not agreed with his main arguments. This is true of Weiser,[76] whose section on Joshua criticizes Noth in these terms: 'The passages of importance for distinguishing the strands Noth explains mostly as additions largely of unknown origin. Thus his attempted solution, which confined itself too much to considerations of pure literary and form-criticism, is confronted with fresh unsolved problems.'[77] So too Eissfeldt,[78] who after recording Noth's approach, simply restates his previous view without argument: 'The book of Joshua tells of the fulfilment of the promise, repeatedly made to the fathers, that the land of Canaan should fall to their descendants (Gen. 13:14–17; 15:7, 18; 17:8; 26:3–4; etc.), and in this respect it is united in content with the Pentateuch. But there is more to it than this. The individual narrative strands combined in it are also connected in style with the Pentateuch, in other words with the narrative strands there combined. So the joining together of the five books of Moses and the book of Joshua as the "Hexateuch" is not merely justified, but is indeed essential for the recognition of the present state of the material.'[79] Weiser restates the familiar J, E, D, P account of the genesis of the book;[80] and Eissfeldt his more distinctive L, J, E, D, P view.[81] Both deal very briefly with the end of Numbers. Weiser sees JE material sharing with P in Num. 32, while Num. 33–36 are secondary appendices.[82] Eissfeldt first attributes everything following Num. 25:6 to P, with the exception of chapter 32 whose material is drawn from LJEP. Later he notes that Num. 28–30 are additions to P; and we may infer that no similar claim is made for the final chapters.[83]

Of subsequent scholars, Anderson[84] is perhaps typical. He offers a cautious welcome to Noth's insights, denying to J the first chapter of Judges and the related material in Joshua,[85] but representing in his discussion of Joshua as a whole—and especially the 'P' material in the second half—a position more like that of Noth's first edition than his second.[86] He too attributes to P everything following Num. 25:6, apart from chapter 32 in which he sees material from J.

Of scholars still working, Fohrer[87] is quite distinctive in his adherence to a view which at least in the matter of the literary sources is that of the older Smend,[88] Simpson[89] and Eissfeldt. His account of the end of Numbers, Joshua, and the first chapter of Judges is heavily dependent on Mowinckel.[90] Indeed he is quite uncritical of the detail in Mowinckel's argument, and merely reattributes Mowinckel's J-material to his own N[91] and divides Mowinckel's J^v-material between his J and E. Noth's analysis is to be rejected as 'oversimplified', one example being its elimination in Jos. 2–6 of 'the verses to be ascribed to E and other doublets as later editorial additions'. Num. 28–31, 33–36 are attributed to P, which Fohrer describes as an independent intellectual unit. This judgment does not, however, eliminate the problem of its literary unity.[92]

Soggin's volume offers no real advance on the discussion in his Commentary.[93] He contrasts the fragmentary account of the conquest by J or the 'collector' with the unitary account which became official and canonical. 'Everything seems to indicate' that this latter (Jos. 1–12) was anticipated by 'a pre-Deuteronomistic redaction, which immediately makes one think of E, but it is impossible to go beyond conjecture pure and simple'.[94] As for the end of Numbers, Soggin too notes that chapters 33–36 are only traditionally attributed to P: they are independent geographical material, certainly parallel to Jos. 13–21.[95]

Lastly Kaiser offers a very sensitive account of the situation in Joshua, leaving us to choose between Mowinckel and Noth until a new analysis appears.[96] 'Against Mowinckel it must be asked whether the account of the conquest has in fact taken over the geographical sketch of Jud. 1, or just quite simply made use of the normal orientation. In respect of Noth's interpretation . . . it remains to be seen whether its literary critical foundation will last.' After a brief review of the problem of Jos. 13–21 he wisely concludes that a decision must be 'based on literary criticism as well as on traditio-historical method'. As for the end of Numbers, Kaiser is alone in following Noth: J told of the settlement and is represented in Num. 32. Deuteronomy was inserted between Num. 27 (or 32*J) and Deut. 34. 'It was only then that Num. 32–35 received their present form, to link together the two historical works which were originally separated from one another.'[97]

It will be the business of the remainder of this study to expose several sections of the book of Joshua and of the end of the book of Numbers to thorough re-examination: in order to test some of the arguments which have already been reviewed; and in order to furnish evidence for a new approach—in fact, to offer the new analysis awaited by Kaiser.

NOTES

1. For a fuller discussion of this problem, see Chapter IV below.
2. *Josua*², pp. 96–97.
3. *op. cit.*, pp. 99–100.
4. 'Boundary and Province Lists' (1956).
5. Ephraimite towns of the far north are combined with the fortress town of En-gedi deep in the Judahite wilderness.
6. Noth had observed this, but argued that the gap was secondarily created for Dan by the redactor.
7. Jehoshaphat, successor to Asa, son of Abijah, they date to *c.* 873–849 B.C.; he is reported in 2 Chron. 17:2 as having garrisoned some of the annexed cities.
8. 'Town Lists' (1958). This happens to be the only study in this section noted by Mowinckel in *T-P-H* (pp. 63, 71).
9. The version of Jos. 21 including Dan (without Beth-Shemesh) seems to be a literary compromise along the lines of the general set-up in the book of Joshua in its final edition, which reflects a restoration of Dan.
10. The original Benjaminite settlements of Gibeah, Anathoth, Azmaveth, Alemeth, and probably also Geba of Benjamin and others of this area are surprisingly absent from Jos. 18:21–28.
11. Mentioned in 2 Chron. 13.
12. While it is possible that the territory of Gezer could have changed extent since the days of Milkilu, the area under discussion is still the natural hinterland of the town.
13. Kallai does admit that Dan is a variation on this theme.
14. His *nḥlwt šbṭy yśr'l* (1967). A fuller summary of this work is offered in English by B. Oded in *Immanuel* 1 (1972), pp. 19–20.
15. *IEJ* 27 (1977), p. 109.
16. 'The province list of Judah' (1959).
17. He remarks it is only for Joseph that a town list is completely lacking.
18. He had earlier observed that when Cross and Wright deemed Bethel and

Ophrah to belong to the same Judahite province as Jericho and Beth-arabah, they succumbed to the very 'nonsense of geography' with which they charged Noth.

19. A useful 'visual aid' in studying Aharoni's views are the informative maps in the Macmillan Bible Atlas (1968), of whose OT section Aharoni was editor.
20. He does remark that a seventh tribe is mentioned at the end of Jud. 1—Dan. However the cities exerting pressure on Dan later came under the influence of Ephraim and Benjamin and were assigned to these tribes.
21. In his paper in *VT* 19, pp. 137ff., where he identifies Rabbah with a previously unidentified *tell* within the confines of the Latrun monastery.
22. He cites in support Jos. 10:40; 11:2, 16; 12:8.
23. As a parallel phenomenon he cites the movement of Ether and Ashan from the end of the Negeb list (Jos. 19:7) to one in the Shephelah (Jos. 15:42).
24. BZAW 86 (1963).
25. Schunck's study offers a wealth of detailed commentary on the studies we have just been reviewing. In this respect it represents a fine introduction to much of the scholarly discussion of the tribal geography in the book of Joshua. The paragraph that follows is no review of this interesting work; it merely samples two arguments of a type that Aharoni could well have used, and yet which point to conclusions radically different from his.
26. What is agreed is that the borders in Jos. 15–19 are derivative in part from the borders of Canaan as described in Num. 34:3–12. However, while Aharoni understands Judah's territory to be defined as everything south of the southernmost border of the northern confederacy, Schunck claims that the borders common to Judah and Benjamin, and Benjamin and Ephraim, are dependent on records of actual frontiers of the state of Judah.
27. 'The Cities of the Territory of Dan' (1960).
28. The first had been the territory of Dan occupied during the conquest of Canaan; in the second, the struggle for mastery had continued till the time of David (the situation there being mirrored in Jud. 1).
29. Additions to Israelite territory at the expense of the Philistines.
30. 'The Inheritance of Dan' (1966).
31. Strange suggests that the whole complex of town lists and boundary descriptions in Jos. 13–19 got its shape and final edition in his reign and on his initiative—they had served to legitimate Josiah's territorial claims when the Assyrian empire began to collapse.
32. *Geographical and Topographical Texts* (1959).
33. It is clear to him (*op. cit.*, p. 114) that Num. 32:33–42 represents a stage in Israel's occupation of Transjordan different from and probably earlier than that presented in other Biblical texts.
34. This question will be more fully discussed in our next chapter.
35. *ZDPV* 89 (1973), pp. 1ff.
36. *ThR* 27, pp. 1–32, 97–146.
37. *KS* IV, pp. 238ff. Eissfeldt's earlier position is described on pp. 46–47 below.
38. *ZAW* 56, pp. 238ff.
39. *VT* 1, pp. 181ff.
40. *ZAW* 72, pp. 107ff.
41. *Ladeheiligtum*, especially pp. 21ff.
42. *Biblica* 66, pp. 125ff.
43. *ThZ* 21, pp. 260ff.
44. *VT Suppl.* 15, pp. 263ff.
45. *Gilgal* (1969).
46. *Early History of Israel*, p. 603.
47. The translation here is that of D. Smith except that it restores de Vaux's use of

'materials' and 'elements' which the translator has transposed (French original, p. 555).

48. *RB* 78, pp. 5–17, 161–183, 321–354.
49. *RB* 79, pp. 7–38.
50. *Transitions in Biblical Scholarship* (1968), pp. 43ff.
51. *Dramatization of Salvific History* . . . (1969).
52. *Svensk Exegetisk Årsbok* 36, pp. 5ff.
53. *Mazzotfest*, pp. 26–103.
54. *Probleme Biblischer Theologie* (1971), pp. 494ff.
55. *Deuteronomium 1:1–6:3*, pp. 95–115.
56. *Untersuchungen zu den siedlungsgeographischen Texten des Alten Testaments. I Ostjordanland* (1975).
57. *Die Hexateucherzählung* (1976).
58. *Das überliefergungsgeschichtliche Problem des Pentateuch* (1977).
59. *Interpreter's Bible.*
60. In the New Century Bible.
61. In the Cambridge Bible Commentary.
62. *Josua* ([2]1958).
63. ATD 9.
64. *Interpreter's Bible.*
65. May, in the new *Peake's Commentary*, is exceptional in offering a more traditional documentary analysis of the book of Joshua, i.e. in terms of J, E, D, and P.
66. In the New Century Bible.
67. *op. cit.*, p. 17.
68. Translated in the OTL series; the work was published first in French in the Commentaire de l'Ancien Testament, 1970.
69. *op. cit.*, p. 3.
70. *op. cit.*, p. 11.
71. Soggin makes no mention of 6:25—see our discussion above, p. 27.
72. Above, p. 29.
73. Mowinckel apparently saw J as having been more expansively 'varied' on the subject of settlement than on earlier topics in the Pentateuch.
74. Cambridge Bible Commentary on the New English Bible.
75. Kaufmann's views on Joshua are more readily available in English in his *Biblical Account* (1953).
76. The first German edition of his *Einleitung* was published in 1948; the English translation is from the 4th edition of 1957.
77. *Introduction*, pp. 146–147.
78. Eissfeldt first published his *Einleitung* in 1934; the English translation is from the 3rd edition of 1964. But of even greater significance for our understanding of Eissfeldt's attitude to the sources of Joshua (as of the Pentateuch as a whole) is his earlier *Hexateuch-Synopse* (1922).
79. *Introduction*, p. 250.
80. *op. cit.*, pp. 144–147.
81. *op. cit.*, pp. 251–257. Eissfeldt offered a specific refutation of Noth's theses soon after their publication, in (a) 'Die Geschichtswerke im AT' (1947), and (b) *Geschichtsschreibung im Alten Testament* (1948). There he argues that the earlier Pentateuchal sources must extend beyond the book of Joshua, and into a description of the period of at least the early monarchy—*only so* could the 'all Israel' reference of their earlier sections be explained, for they had anachronistically read back into the early history a political situation only created in the monarchy. (Eissfeldt's assumption appears very weak—other accounts could and have been offered.)

82. *op. cit.*, p. 136.
83. *op. cit.*, p. 189, 195, 200–201, 205.
84. *Critical Introduction* (1959).
85. *op. cit.*, p. 66.
86. *op. cit.*, pp. 59–61.
87. Fohrer's *Introduction* (1970) is a translation of the 10th edition of Sellin's *Einleitung* (1965) which Fohrer had completely revised and reshaped.
88. *Erzählung des Hexateuch* (1912).
89. *Early Traditions* (1948).
90. Fohrer, pp. 198–199; the section on Joshua as a whole is in pp. 196–205.
91. His 'Nomadic' source which contains largely the material of Smend's J^1 and Eissfeldt's L.
92. *Introduction*, pp. 180, 182.
93. *Introduction*, pp. 161–174. (The Italian original was first published in 1967.) In fact the parallels in Joshua with Jud. 1 are listed less accurately on p. 169 than on p. 13 of the earlier commentary.
94. *op. cit.*, p. 170.
95. *op. cit.*, p. 144.
96. *Introduction* (1975), pp. 134–142. The German original was first published in 1969.
97. *op. cit.*, p. 107.

CHAPTER IV

THE DISTRIBUTION OF THE LAND IN JOSHUA

A. A Fresh Approach

Three principal factors have caused the problems faced by critics in their analyses of Jos. 13–22. Two of these have been amply illustrated in the preceding three chapters: the complexity of the text itself; and the weight of inherited critical presuppositions. The third has been lack of attention to the history of the transmission of the text of the book of Joshua.

Accordingly, what will be offered here will be the first stages of a *relative* literary stratification of the material in these chapters—an account of the interrelationships and development of the different sections of the text which forswears at the outset any labelling of the strata on the basis of inherited conclusions from other texts. This means accepting the challenge of Engnell's slogan 'consistently traditio-historical'[1]—and interpreting it quite radically as implying a starting-point in the *different forms* in which we have received the tradition. To be specific: we must first take account of the quality of our Hebrew (MT) and Greek (LXX) texts as witnesses to the common tradition of Joshua from which both derive.

In a number of recent studies[2] I have sought to demonstrate (a) that at least at some recurring points of difference the LXX attests a parent Hebrew tradition certainly anterior to that of the MT, while at others its differing testimony should enjoy the benefit of the doubt; and (b) that this recognition must influence literary decisions about the production of the text. The argument that follows will recall some of the results already published, and will—when the texts differ—generally make the Greek the basis for further discussion of the second half of Joshua.[3]

B. The Introduction

Smend's 'contribution to the history of Deuteronomistic redaction'[4] has already been mentioned. His paper reviews the evidence in Joshua and the beginning of Judges for a series of homogeneous additions to the basic Deuteronomistic text (DtrG) that may be assigned to a 'nomistic' hand that produced a second edition of the Deuteronomistic History (DtrN).[5] Smend argues that the original extent of the opening divine address to Joshua had been Jos. 1:1–6, concluding with a specific demand for courage in face of the task of settlement. The final three verses of the address interpret this demand as a call to meditate continuously on Yahweh's commands and remember all Moses' instructions (v. 7), locate these specifically in the book of the Law (v. 8), and by their use in v. 9 of vocabulary from v. 6 and even v. 5 ease the transition to v. 10 and indicate that it was not the intention of the interpolator to abrogate the original meaning.

It is in his discussion of 13:1b–6 that Smend broaches the question whose answer is critical not only for his own immediately following topic (Jos. 23) but also for our present chapter. He agrees with Noth[6] that both references to Joshua's advanced age (in 13:1a and 23:1b) cannot belong to the same stratum of the book. Noth had felt the reference appropriate just before the account of Joshua's final address. Smend finds it more likely that a secondary editor has repeated this material at a later and even more suitable point in the narrative, than that a phrase which originally belonged to the very last stage in the story was secondarily reapplied to an earlier and so inherently less suitable stage. His next observation is that Jos. 13 opens with several parallels to the beginning of the book: Both open with a formal notice. Both follow this immediately with a divine address that restates this notice—'Moses my servant is dead; now therefore . . .' (1:2); 'You are old and advanced in years, . . .' (13:1). The parallelism of the divine addresses in these chapters would be even more remarkable if 13:7, opening with 'now therefore (*wʿth*)', were read immediately after the words quoted from v. 1.

> What presently separates these verses is a rather long passage that deals with the land (more precisely with the continuing incompleteness of its conquest) listing a whole series of geographical details.[7] The transition at its conclusion is clumsy, and the beneficiaries differ:
>
> v. 6b: *rḳ hplh lyśr'l bnḥlh k'šr ṣwytyk*
>
> v. 7: *wʿth ḥlḳ 't-h'rṣ hz't bnḥlh ltšʿt hšbṭym . . .*
>
> —Israel in v. 6, and the nine and a half Cisjordanian tribes in v. 7. There is a difference too in the land divided: in v. 7 it is Palestine west of the Jordan, just conquered; in v. 6 the suffix in *hplh* refers back to *h'rṣ hnš'rt* mentioned in v. 2a and specified in vv. 2b–6a. And this focuses our attention on the similar clumsiness of transition from v. 1 to v. 2. Smend argues that the closing phrase of v. 1 was part of the original divine address to Joshua: *wh'rṣ nš'rh . . . lršth* (although not the strengthening *hrbh-m'd*[8]). If he is correct, the reference is to the land mentioned also in v. 7; and what is here noted is that, while it is conquered, it still remains for active ownership to be entered into. By contrast, the 'remaining land' of v. 2 is land not yet conquered.

We see that the method of the interpolator of vv. 2–6 is identical to that of 1:7–9—he linked his insertion to a significant phrase in the text before him which he either misunderstood or deliberately re-interpreted.[9] The law is close to the heart of the interpolator in chapter 1; the incompleteness of the settlement and the continued existence of foreigners in the land, to the one in chapter 13.

Smend notes the close relation of these interests in the next text he analyzes, Jos. 23.[10] The relevant parts of this chapter cannot be detached from the whole as was the case with 1:7–9 and 13:2–6. Rather the whole chapter provides the clue to the better understanding of these earlier insertions, and shows them to have been elements of a comprehensive edition (DtrN). As with them, so here the immediately preceding Deuteronomistic passage (in this case 21:43–45) provides the point of departure for the account. There are several linguistic links; yet, on closer attention, important differences too: While 21:44b stated, 'not one of all their enemies had withstood them . . .', 23:9b notes with greater reserve, 'not one has withstood you to this day'. Then our chapter distinguishes two kinds of 'peoples' (not 'enemies' as in 21:44 and 23:1). With the one, Yahweh has dealt in the past, before Israel's eyes (23:3). But there are also those that remain, whose territory is already allotted to the Israelites and whom Yahweh will drive out as he has promised (23:5). Verse 13, however, makes plain that such support will not continue if the Israelites mix with them and worship their gods. 21:45 has talked of the fulfilment of Yahweh's good word; 23:14b–16 lay alongside this his bad word which will just as surely be fulfilled should Israel transgress the divine assignment. Smend thus vindicates Noth's first reaction to Jos. 23–24[11]: that Jos. 24 was the earlier and the pattern for Jos. 23. DtrN was not concerned to replace the earlier text (which can now be claimed as an integral part of DtrG); once he had shown the relevance of its main assertion to his own time he was happy to let it stand, even if only as something of an appendix.[12]

Further elements of Smend's argument will be discussed later. Suffice it to add for the moment that his analysis of Joshua has been complemented by Dietrich's monograph[13] arguing that the Deuteronomistic edition of Kings was accomplished in *three* stages—he interposes an edition specifically concerned with prophecy (DtrP) between Noth's pioneer DtrG and Smend's DtrN. A rather different account of two Deuteronomists in Kings has been offered by Cross and adopted by Boling in his commentary on Judges in the Anchor Bible.[14]

Wüst's *Untersuchungen*[15] offer a very different account of Jos. 13:1–7. He is surprisingly silent over Smend's article. He follows Noth in seeing the core of 13:1ff. as a link (drawing on 23:1) between the main Deuteronomist's report of the taking of the land in the first half of Joshua and the once separate traditions of its distribution in chapters 14–19.

Since the significant details in these verses have already been mentioned in our report of Smend's argument, the main points of Wüst's case can be more briefly presented:

(a) The original continuation of Jos. 13:1 is v. 6b not v. 7. That latter verse with its mention of the nine and a half tribes functions as a transition from vv. 1, 6b with their interest (like chapters 14–19) in the land west of the Jordan to vv. 8ff. which recapitulate the Transjordanian situation.[16]

(b) Much hangs on the exact meaning of the final clause in 13:1. Those who added the following verses clearly *mis*understand it as referring to land within wide ideal borders, which Jos. 1–12 had not reported as conquered. Noth (and Holzinger before him) had assumed that the original drafter of our verse agreed with the Deuteronomist's summary statements in Jos. 10:40 and 11:16 that the whole land had been militarily taken or conquered, and noted here that real possession was far from fully entered on. Such a distinction between *lkḥ* or *hkh* there and *yrš* here is for Wüst impermissible: *yrš* is used alongside and in the same sense as one of the other verbs in question in several passages in Numbers, Deuteronomy, and Joshua.[17] And even the possible distinction between *lkḥ* in Deut. 3:8 and *yrš* in 3:12 provides no backing for Noth's assumption, since this passage is later than Jos. 1[18]—and may even represent a similar misreading of it to Noth's. One must simply observe that our verse is not from the main Deuteronomistic stratum of Joshua, and that it expresses a different view from 10:40 and 11:16 about the completeness of the occupation.

This appears a bad argument for a number of reasons. Firstly it is quite appropriate for terms to be used as broad synonyms in one context, yet have their distinctive emphases brought out in another. Next, even Wüst's account of Deut. 3 shows that a distinction between our two verbs was not impossible for a classical Hebrew reader. And finally, all the passages he quotes against Noth mention taking/conquering and (fully) possessing in the context of *summary* prospects of the settlement or *brief* retrospects of the settlement in Transjordan. For all the conciseness of expression, the verbs can still be held to enshrine distinct aspects of the total settlement process.

Smend's account of Jos. 13:1–7 is to be preferred to Wüst's. Smend also offers a simpler account of the relationship between Jos. 13:2–6 and parts of Jos. 23: they all belong to the same secondary Deuteronomistic stratum. Wüst however sees 13:6a as inspired by 23:3; but 23:4a derived from 13:6b. Just one further element of his argument should be noted here: since he finds the continuation of Jos. 13:1 in v. 6b, the idea of dividing the land *by lot* is deemed implicit in this basic stratum (*hplh* of v. 6b), and a link detected between this stratum and the core of Jos. 18:3–10. However good reason will be shown below why the original stratum (Smend's 13:1, 7) does not mention lot as the principle of division.

For our present purposes, however, we shall forego the use of Smend's labels (DtrG[19] and DtrN). Some of the arguments advanced by Mittmann and Wüst about the development of the opening chapters of Deuteronomy[20] may require a reconsideration of such terminology. But his demonstration that Jos. 1:7–9; 13:2–6; and 23 represent modifications to 1:1–6; 13:1, 7; and 21:43–45; 24; and his observation that 13:1, 7, is structured like 1:1–6 appear a reliable 'contribution to the history of Deuteronomistic reduction'.

C. A Second Introduction?

I have argued elsewhere[21] that we do best justice to the complexities of the apparent second introduction to the distribution of the land in Joshua by recognizing that 14:1–5 has been drafted in three stages: v. 1a—an introduction to the west-Jordan (Canaan) distribution; vv. 1b–3—an expansion and correction of this; and vv. 4–5—a further explanation. The separation of the second and third stages is indicated in part by changes in terminology, and that of the first two by a very awkward Hebrew sentence. Wüst's analysis[22] is similar but even more complex.

If the core of Jos. 14:1–5 is simply v. 1a (*w'lh 'šr-nḥlw bny-yśr'l b'rṣ kn'n*) then what is its function? The form of words is not usual[23] but is closely paralleled in the (almost) adjoining 13:32—*'lh 'šr-nḥl mšh b'rbwt mw'b.*[24] That verse concludes the specification in 13:15ff. of the details of Moses' Transjordanian allocation, already outlined in vv. 8–12. No other piece of territory is described twice in this way in Jos. 13–19.[25] And vv. 15ff. give every impression of being a supplement to the preceding verses in the spirit of the chapters that follow.[26] Accordingly Jos. 13:32; 14:1a function as a transition from the inserted material back to the theme introduced at the beginning of chapter 13—the division of Cisjordan.

The gradual expansion of the opening of chapter 14 shows that it came to be treated as the main introduction to the material in Jos. 15–19. However we have good reason to believe that 13:1, 7 earlier served this function.[27]

D. The Principle of Lot in Jos. 13–17

One of the implications of this short account of Jos. 14:1–5 demands immediate scrutiny—that 'lot' (*gwrl*) is mentioned explicitly in the introductory material to the account of the Cisjordanian distribution only in an addition to an addition to the introduction. It will be remembered that one result of our decision above for Smend against Wüst that the original continuation of 13:1 was to be found in 13:7 not 13:6b was that the earliest introductory stratum bore no implication even of distribution by lot.

These literary conclusions support and are themselves supported by the witness of the LXX in the opening verses of each of Jos. 15–17. In all three opening verses the Greek attests *gbwl* (territory/border), and not *gwrl* as in MT. This divergence between the nouns is not confined to these chapters, but reappears twice in Jos. 21[28] where a Hebrew parallel in Chronicles[29] adds to the weight of the Greek evidence. In the MT of Joshua, it is only in these five disputed verses that *gwrl* means allotted portion/allotment and not simply a lot cast or drawn.[30] *gbwl* makes as good sense, brings the introductory comments on the territory of Judah, Joseph, and Manasseh into line with what is said (in both MT and LXX) of Ephraim in 16:5, and requires no meaning for *gwrl* unusual in Joshua.

In the Greek book of Joshua, 'lot' is mentioned specifically only in 14:2 within Jos. 13–17. This late addition may well have been the inspiration for the emendations in our familiar Hebrew tradition. But its lateness in the introductory material and its absence from the best text of the descriptions themselves leave us free to glimpse more accurately the intention of the earlier drafters of these accounts of land division.

E. Half-Manasseh

The material edited in the second half of Joshua is certainly very diverse. Sensitive literary criticism and attention to the more reliable Greek testimony to the text may help one penetrate some of the complexities. Yet some erratic boulders protrude further than their fellows, and some of these have to do with the half-tribe of Manasseh east of the Jordan.

(1) Half-Manasseh in Jos. 13–17:

Within Jos. 13, the relative regularity of the structure of the sections on Reuben (vv. 15–23) and Gad (vv. 24–28) only serves to underline the difference from both of the section on half-Manasseh (vv. 29–31). Its content is much more general. And instead of their formal conclusion—*z't nḥlt bny r'wbn/gd lmšpḥtm*—it ends with the pleonastic *lbny mkyr bn-mnšh lḥṣy-bny-mkyr lmšpḥtm.*[31] It is unlikely that these three verses were drafted along with the sections on Reuben and Gad.

The introduction to the (other) Manassite holding in Jos. 17 is quite the most complex of all. All the more or less regular features of an introduction can be culled from vv. 1, 2, and 7. *wyhy hgbwl lmṭh mnšh* (1) . . . *lmšpḥtm* (2) . . . *m'šr* (7)[32] provides a similar general orientation for Manasseh as *wyhy hgbwl lmṭh bny yhwdh lmšpḥtm 'l-gbwl 'dwm* in 15:1 for Judah. However the considerable intervening material in 17:1–6 gives every impression of having grown rather than been planned.

Manasseh is no sooner mentioned in the introduction than two comments are made: that he is Joseph's elder son; and that Machir, his elder son, has received Gilead and Bashan.[33] This prompts a new start in v. 2—*wyhy lbny mnšh hnwtrym.* These remaining sons are all then named, and the resuming comment prepares the way for the next surprise by noting that these were but Manasseh's remaining male children. The problem of Zelophehad's five daughters, familiar also from Num. 27 and 36, is then mentioned (vv. 3–4), and vv. 5–6 offer a rather pleonastic summary of Manasseh's situation as so far described. Some inconsistencies of terminology should be noted, which may be significant for the stratification of these verses:

(a) Manasseh's Transjordanian territory is referred to variously as *hgl'd whbšn* in v. 1; *'rṣ hgl'd whbšn* in v. 5; and *'rṣ hgl'd* in v. 6.[34]

(b) The phrase *lbny mnšh hnwtrym* refers to the Cisjordanian clans in v. 2, but to the Transjordanian ones in v. 6.

It is not our purpose here to offer a detailed account of the development of Jos. 17:1–7. The information these verses offer is more extensive than the extra notes in 18:11b or 19:1b which observe that Benjamin was between Judah and Joseph or Simeon within Judah; and unlike these notes our verses interrupt rather than complement the more or less regular structure. It is difficult not to conclude that an earlier draft of the traditions in Jos. 15–17 described the territory of Manasseh (or Machir) like that of Ephraim—two neighbours in the central highlands—and paid no heed to (reputedly) related clans in Gilead (and Bashan).

(2) Half-Manasseh in Jos. 22:

This chapter describes the dispatch of the Transjordanians after the completion of conquest and distribution (vv. 1–6) and the resultant problem between east and west of the Jordan over an altar sacred to the Transjordanians. The position of half-Manasseh in both parts of this chapter is anomalous.

In v. 1, *lr'wbny wlgdy* is followed in the normally best MSS by *wlḥṣy mṭh mnšh*. Some MSS have *šbṭ* in the answering phrase, as is almost regular after the patronymic forms for Reuben and Gad. It could be that this is the original reading and that *mṭh* of the best witnesses has been influenced by the use of that term in Jos. 21; but the fact stands that these MSS describe the two and a half Transjordanian tribes in a unique phrase. Then, while the altar-story proper talks of the Transjordanians returning to 'the land of Gilead' (vv. 9, 13, 32), an apparently gratuitous note in v. 7 talks of Manasseh being settled half in *Bashan* and half with its brothers in the west (somewhat analogous to the contorted explanations in 17:1ff.). In the light of our observations on Manasseh in Jos. 13 and 17, it is likely that the original function of 22:7 was to reinforce the recruitment of half Manasseh to the eastern tribes—a recruitment that occurred after the first drafting of the altar story.[35]

In that story, unlike the brief account of their prior dispatch, the two tribes are specified throughout as *bny r'wbn* and *bny gd*. Yet three different phrases are used in the MT for half-Manasseh: (i) *ḥṣy šbṭ hmnšh* in vv. 9, 10, 11, 21; (ii) *ḥṣy šbṭ mnšh* in vv. 13, 15; and (iii) *bny-mnšh* in vv. 30, 31. And equally remarkable, in the MT the two tribes are mentioned on their own in vv. 32, 33, 34—and in v. 25.[36] The situation in the LXX is no clearer: on the one hand, it is characteristically shorter on the whole than the MT; on the other, it mentions half-Manasseh also in vv. 32–34—in fact every time it mentions Reuben and Gad. And while its testimony confirms the regularity of phrase for detailing these two tribes[37] its terminology for the half tribe varies in a quite different pattern from the Hebrew. The evidence of both MT and LXX could be accounted for by a hypothesis of inconsistent and independent supplementation of both versions of the tradition.[38]

Our cautious conclusion is that we may have evidence that an earlier version of the problem of the altar featured only Reuben and Gad after their return to Gilead; that half-Manasseh was added to our chapter with some deliberation (v. 7)—but the detailed implications were only slowly drawn; and that the *Hebrew* textual uncertainty in v. 1 is capable of the same explanation.

(3) Half-Manasseh elsewhere in Joshua:

The other brief references to the half tribe form two groups. We find a summary mention of the two and a half Transjordanian tribes as a unit in 1:12; 4:12; 12:6; 13:7; 18:7; and 20:8—this concept conforms to the account of the conquest of Transjordan in Deut. 2–3, and to the only other such summary mention in the Former Prophets (2 Kings 10:33). Then the two half tribes are listed in other groupings in the account of Levitical cities (21:5, 6, 25, 27). One suspects that the relative independence of the half tribe in Jos. 21 marks a stage in the tradition later than its presence with Reuben and Gad as one of the Transjordanian group. It is these earlier summary references that deserve further scrutiny.

In principle they *could* all[39] have had half-Manasseh added to them as in Jos. 22; or they might all reflect a concept of two and a half tribes in the east which caused adjustment to be made to any traditions which spoke only of Reuben and Gad across the Jordan, or a united Manasseh in the west. At one of these passages—Jos. 13:7–8—MT and LXX offer strikingly different testimony. The one thing they could be said to agree over is lack of symmetry with which both mention the two tribes and the half tribe: In the brief MT, *'mw* at first sight refers back to *western* half-Manasseh of the antecedent nine and a half tribes; but as the following *hr'wbny whgdy* makes clear 'with it' is a forced reference to the half tribe in the east. Then in the uncharacteristically fuller LXX, the phrase 'the two tribes and the half tribe of Manasseh' is followed by the parenthetic 'Reuben and Gad'. I have already published a defence of the LXX in this passage.[40] It is that version which may contain the evidence that even it does not represent the first draft of the passage:

> Now divide this land for settlement[41]
> *to the nine tribes and the half tribe of Manasseh.*
> From the Jordan to the great sea at the setting of the sun you will make grant of it—
> it is the great sea that will be the frontier.
> *To the two tribes and the half tribe of Manasseh*
> to Reuben and Gad Moses made a grant across the Jordan to the east.
> Moses servant of Yahweh granted them from Aroer . . .

An attractive text is 'restored' if the two phrases italicized in the above translation are deleted. It is certainly only in this passage and in the late and related Num. 34:13 and Jos. 14:2 that the western tribes are referred to as 'the nine and a half tribes'.[42]

These observations have two results: they suggest that the beginning of Jos. 13 was supplemented, as we already suspected of its end; and they leave us with only four verses[43] which lack remarkable features to discuss, and which can be accommodated to the hypothesis just developed.

F. Joseph

Chapters 16 and 17 of the book of Joshua begin and end with Joseph; but most of what they have to say is about Ephraim and Manasseh. These two tribes are seen as subdivisions of the other; or else Joseph brackets them together. The concept of the final editor is more or less clear; and it is almost as clear that the (bulk of the) 'raw' information in these chapters concerned Ephraim and Manasseh separately. What falls to be discussed in this section is whether there is evidence that an earlier draft of these traditions concerned itself only with Ephraim and Manasseh, and what the implications would be for the development of Jos. 13–19 as a whole.

One point at issue is just how completely the borders of Joseph, Ephraim, and Manasseh are described. Simons as always makes a brave attempt to attribute sensible meaning to the text as it stands.[44] His translation and commentary depict (1) a southern boundary of Joseph—16:1–3; (2) a southern and northern (more properly, north-eastern and north-western) boundary of Ephraim—16:5–8a; (3) an indication of Manasseh's northern extent—17:7a, and a description of the western part of its southern border shared with Ephraim—17:7b–9; (4) the western and northern extent of Ephraim and Manasseh (i.e. Joseph)—17:10. Cities of Ephraim and Manasseh are mentioned in 16:9–10 and 17:11–13; and the most acute problem for Simons' analysis is whether 17:10 is really intended to describe Joseph's western and northern limit or Manasseh's.

The relevant part of the verse reads as follows (Simons here accepts the Greek testimony): *whyh hym gbwlm wb'šr ypg'wn mṣpwn wbyšškr mmzrḥ*. Certainly the antecedent of the suffix in *gbwlm* and the subject of *ypg'wn* is not the singular *gbwl* (*mnšh*) of vv. 7–9. Yet no more is it *hgbwl lbny ywsp* of 16:1. The nearest candidates in the present text as referents for these plurals in v. 10 are supplied in the first four words of the verse which conclude v. 9's account of the *nḥl ḳnh* as the border between Ephraim and Manasseh: *ngbh l'prym wṣpwnh lmnšh*. And so Simons reads the remainder of the verse as describing the limits of not just Manasseh but Ephraim-and-Manasseh or Joseph. That appears to me to be far-fetched. If I felt constrained to see in 17:10 the conclusion of what was begun in 16:1–3 I should prefer to see *bny ywsp* of 16:1 as the referent of the problem plurals. Yet, if one is again prepared to give the Greek the benefit of the doubt, there is a similar but closer antecedent in 17:7—*wyhy gbwl bny mnšh m'šr*.[45]

One problem for Simons' reading has already been hinted at: the tribes Asher and Issachar are used to define the extent of the territory described in v. 10 and they appear again in v. 11 as areas in which Manasseh had rights. It seems not unlikely that the author of v. 11 understood v. 10 also to be defining Manasseh's holding, not Joseph's. According to this reading, we finish with Manasseh (vv. 1–13) before returning to Joseph (vv. 14–18).

It has already been suggested that the source-material for our chapters described Ephraim and Manasseh separately. It is an editor of Jos. 16–17 who treated this joint territory as that of Joseph (rather than divided Joseph's area by describing Ephraim's and Manasseh's common border through it). If our preferred reading of 17:10 is correct, separate accounts of Ephraim and Manasseh—though brief—have been preserved in their integrity. And there are two indications that these two border descriptions represent the same literary stratum as most others in Jos. 15–19, while that in 16:1–3 is different—and so probably later. One is that both have the regular *lmšpḥtm* ('family by family') in their introductions (16:5 and 17:2), while it is lacking in 16:1. And the other is that the descriptions of Ephraim (16:7) and Manasseh (17:10) share with those of the four tribes further to the north (19:11, 22, 26, 27, 34) the only occurrences of *pg' b-* ('touch') in a territorial sense.

There are at least grounds then for supposing that the main drafting of border descriptions in Jos. 15–19 detailed Ephraim and Manasseh, but not

Joseph. It has long been discussed whether their present order is the original one. It is striking that both Jos. 14:4 and 16:4 (MT) talk of Manasseh and Ephraim as the constituent parts of Joseph—and in 16:4 this harder reading is perhaps to be preferred to LXX's Ephraim and Manasseh.[46] That the MT 'plus' in 17:17 mentions Ephraim and Manasseh according to the present order of the two chapters is straightforward. We may suppose that 14:4 and 16:4 (MT) when they were penned reflected the order of our chapters quite as naturally as 17:17 (MT) when it was later added. And we shall note further evidence below that Manasseh did appear first.[47]

To conclude this section, a word must be said about the closing verses of Jos. 17—if only to show why they cannot be discussed adequately here. The LXX offers a text markedly different from the MT—considerably shorter, and easier to read. It is quite without certain phrases of the MT: *šm b'rṣ hprzy whrp'ym* (v. 15); *bny ywsp* (v. 16); *l'prym wlmnšh* (v. 17); and *tṣ'tyw* (v. 18). Then at the end of v. 14 it offers the shorter 'and *God* has blessed me' for MT's unusual *'d 'šr-'d-kh brkny yhwh.*[48] And at the end of v. 16 both versions present considerable difficulties.[49] In the absence of a thorough study of these different versions, any statement about 17:14–18 must remain tentative. It is often claimed that it preserves an ancient fragment of tradition, like those in Jud. 1. And Alt's opinion is famous, that Joshua is at home in these verses while in much of the book that bears his name his role is a secondary addition to the traditions of settlement and distribution. My own survey of the opening of Judges[50] has led me to wonder just how much ancient information it contains. Certainly our five verses appear in Joshua straight after one of the parallels (17:11–13) to Jud. 1 (vv. 27–28). Then our v. 16, like Jud. 1:19, describes the difficulty of settling in a plain when competing with Canaanites and their iron chariots. Yet Jud. 1:19 seems one of the latest in a late composition. And, while Alt's judgment about Joshua being 'at home' in the story may have merit, the appropriate conclusion may be that the narrative is late—not that we have here a reliable early tradition about Joshua.[51]

G. Lot and Land Commission

It is only in Jos. 18–19 that the reader of the present text of the book recognizes description at all like that promised in 14:1–3—a series of accounts, in an order dictated by lot drawn by Joshua, of areas defined in a territorial survey carried out by his commissioners. His only surprise is in having to wait so long and that a new 'introduction' (18:1–10) should be necessary after three chapters of information. Indeed many critics have argued that this introduction (or at least its core, shorn of the number seven) once stood at the head of the account of land distribution. A variant of this argument is provided by Wüst: that 18:3, 4, 8a, 9*, 10b originally followed 13:1, 6b.[52]

The question such an approach generally fails to answer is just *why* an integral part of the first introduction to the distribution of the land should have been recast and relocated. The motive necessary for that would have been sufficient to inspire either a piece of fresh writing or the import of a tradition not yet associated with the material in the developing book of Joshua. An imaginative attempt to recapture such a motive was made by Vink—although in the context of a somewhat eccentric essay on the date and origin of the Priestly Code.[53] the presentation of the whole account of land distribution in Joshua was an implicit appeal to dispersed Israelites to resettle the land in the Persian period, when the land was at peace (18:1) and there were established (provincial) centres in the south and centre (v. 5), around Jerusalem and Samaria.

The familiar argument, even in Wüst's restatement, is defective on two principal grounds. Firstly, the earlier sections of this chapter have challenged his assertion that there is a gap in the introduction to Jos. 13–19 for 18:1–10 or its kernel to fill. (i) The call to *divide* the land (13:1, 7) is followed quite naturally by a description of various *territories*. (ii) It is the 'territory' (*gbwl*) not 'allotment' (*gwrl*) of each territory that the best text of Joshua described in chapters 15–17. (iii) Talk of lot and land-commission in 14:1b–2 belongs to a late stratum in the tradition. Thus even Wüst's core of 18:1–10 is unsuitable as an opening for Jos. 15–17 so understood. Then one must have considerable textual reservations about his analysis of these verses: MT and LXX repeatedly part company—and the conclusion of his core (v. 10b) is a Hebrew 'plus' in its entirety.

If 18:1–10* belongs ill earlier in the book, it certainly belongs well from some points of view where it stands. It is only in 17:14–18 that the charge in 18:3 is in any way anticipated, that there has been sluggishness or lack of initiative amongst the tribes over the matter of settlement—Joseph is told in 17:15, 18 that if his territory is too constricted he should take over more. Then the immediately following description of the *gbwl* of each of the seven remaining tribes in Jos. 18–19 is introduced by a mention of the drawing of the appropriate *gwrl*—LXX here supports MT in giving each term a distinct function.[54]

The next point to note is that it is the present state of Jos. 16–17 that chapters 18–19 assume. The already existing entities (18:5) are the territory of Judah and territori*es* of Joseph (NB one Joseph, but divided). This is emphasized by the observation concerning Benjamin in 18:11b that its allotted territory was between Judah and Joseph.

As one studies the text and literary relations of 18:1–10 one can readily understand why successive critics assigned v. 1 to the 'Hexateuchal' source P and most of vv. 2–10 to JE. In the text of the LXX, v. 1 is even more readily detachable from what follows: vv. 2–10 in its briefer text are consistent with a scene of action other than Shiloh; if v. 1 represents a new introduction to an earlier anecdote, then the MT pluses 'here' (v. 6) and 'to the camp at Shiloh' (v. 9) attempt to give the narrative a greater unity than the earlier draft preserved in the LXX possessed.

The opening phrase, about the assembly of the whole community of Israel at Shiloh, is found again in Jos. 22:12b, where the assembly takes stock of the news of the Transjordanians' altar. Then the 'Tent of Meeting' (*'hl mw'd*) appears frequently in Exodus-Numbers[55] but seldom elsewhere[56] —and nowhere else is there talk of placing or erecting this Tent. In fact the verb *hškyn* used here occurs only six times in the Hebrew Bible, and nowhere else of pitching a tent. The noun *mškn* occurs in Jos. 22:19, 29 (and governs the Qal verb *škn* in v. 19), referring to an official sanctuary west of the Jordan. A combination of these verses in Jos. 22 with v. 12b already mentioned may have been the inspiration for this unique formulation in 18:1. Its third and last phrase, 'and the land was subdued before them', has only three close parallels: in 1 Chron. 22:18, of the peace prevailing at David's hand-over to Solomon; and in Num. 32:22, 29, where the subjection of the land marks the end of the Transjordanians' obligation to fight with their brothers in the west—a topic similar to that in Jos. 22![57] Together, even if not severally, these considerations make it probable that this verse represents one of the latest strata of the book, and possibly later than vv. 2–10.

In these latter verses, as almost always, the shorter LXX text has its attractions—and not just because some of the differences in the MT can be explained as an attempt to harmonize vv. 2–10 with v. 1. However, especially in vv. 4–6 neither text appears satisfactory.[58] Within the tradition common to both MT and LXX, there are a number of expressions unique to this passage.

Neither expression for casting lots (*yrh* or *hšlyk*) is found elsewhere; and the phrase *khnt yhwh* is otherwise unknown. The few parallels with expressions not appearing elsewhere in the Former Prophets may be instructive. *'d-'nh* (v. 3) is found in a number of contexts.[59] The verb *htrph* (v. 3) occurs only in Prov. 18:9; 24:10—and it is only in Prov. 17:2 that we find a precise parallel to MT's *ḥlkw 't-nḥltm* in v. 2[60]—elsewhere in Numbers-Joshua, *ḥlk* is construed only with *'rṣ* or a suffix assuming it, apart from Jos. 22:8 where its object is 'booty'. Probably the only other passage in which *'md* is used of a people 'holding' its territory is Ex. 8:18, where Goshen is excepted from the plague of flies. Gen. 13:7, where Abraham is ordered to traverse the land he is being given, provides a parallel to *hthlk b'rṣ* (vv. 4, 8). And *'br b'rṣ* (v. 9) can be compared with Gen. 12:6—and perhaps Num. 13:32; 14:7; 20:17; 21:22 (there too with a view to ownership). All this evidence is at least consistent with the anecdote being a late creation.

Verse 7 may repay fuller consideration. Its first part—*ky 'yn-ḥlk llwym bkrbkm ky-khnt yhwh nḥltw*—stands in an oft-repeated Deuteronomic tradition[61] that the Levites have no *ḥlk wnḥlh* within Israel. Where this is cited in Joshua, only one of the nouns is used—*nḥlh* in 13:14 and *ḥlk* in 14:4 and here. The second noun is used in our verse's unique modification of the second part of the tradition, that his portion is Yahweh's priesthood.[62] Then it is only here in the book of Joshua that Gad and Reuben are so referred to—using the simple names, and in that order. The order can be paralleled only in Num. 32.[63] And what is said of them is similarly unusual—the phrase *lkḥw nḥltm* is found only in Num. 34:14, 15 and Jos. 13:8(MT).[64] The passage in Num. 34 is late; and even if the MT were to be preferred in Jos. 13:8 it is hardly the inspiration for our verse with its unconventional naming of the tribes. However the following geographical expression—*m'br lyrdn mzrḥh*—seems to be found only in later strata of Numbers and Joshua.[65]

Thus Jos. 18:7 is a microcosm of our passage as a whole: it contains novel ideas and expressions, and it appears related to later material in associated books. A thorough study of the textual witnesses to vv. 2–10 would be necessary, however, before we could begin to judge how well and in how many stages they were drafted.

We have noted ample ground for the surprise of the reader of Joshua at this new introduction within the story of the distribution of the land. Yet the newcomer has made itself at home—the following story of seven lots depends on it; and it is at least familiar with that other likely newcomer—the house of Joseph. The reader is to a degree prepared for this otherwise sudden appearance of lot and a commission assisting Joshua by the additions made to 14:1a—but their terminology is different, and related to other texts which fall to be discussed below.[66]

H. Corrections

Throughout Jos. 13–19 we come across a series of brief notes that conclude the sections on which they also depend: 13:13; 15:63; 16:10; 17:11–13; and 19:47 (LXX). All of these except the first have close parallels in Jud. 1, and scholars have long held that that chapter (or the source from which it itself is derived) is their source. I have already published an argument that Jud. 1 is in fact based on these and other parts of the book of Joshua; and have offered in that context a full account of the associated text-critical problems of the Joshua notes.[67] It will suffice here to repeat the main conclusions and attempt to draw out the implications for our understanding of the growth of the book of Joshua.

In these verses, the LXX is to be preferred in almost every respect to the MT; it is easier to explain the MT as a development of the LXX than the other way round. By this reckoning, the parallel verses in Jud. 1 are based on a proto-Massoretic form of the text of Joshua. The more original text available to the Greek translators allows us to see that all these notes reckoned with a thorough-going setback to the Israelite settlers' fortunes in the areas in question. The first three notes give instances of pre-Israelite groups that could not be dispossessed but remained as alien enclaves. Only in the last two cases does the tradition common to LXX and MT record some amelioration of the position as the strength of Israel (17:13) or Ephraim (19:47) grew. The MT has softened the impact of two of the earlier notes: (a) into the closing comment of 15:63 that 'the Jebusite lived on in Jerusalem to this day' it has intruded the limiting phrase 'with the people of Judah'; (b) to the conclusion 'the Canaanite lived on in the midst of Ephraim to this day' (16:10) it has appended 'but became subject to forced labour'—perhaps inspired by 17:13 and 19:47.

All five notes share two characteristics: they appear at the end of the sections to which they relate; and they correct their emphasis. All do this by taking issue with a specific piece of information given or implied in the preceding section. All but the last use some form of *l' hwryš* ('did not dispossess'). The first three share the expression *'d hywm hzh* ('to this day'). And each of these aspects of our five notes is a feature of one or more of the three passages attributed by Smend to DtrN and discussed above.[68] This harmony in spirit, method, and language makes it very probable that they too are the work of its editors.[69]

One more substantial addition to Jos. 13–19 is also re-used in Jud. 1—15:13–19. More precisely, Jos. 15:15–19 is almost identical to Jud. 1:11–15. Despite its greater length it lacks the distinctive phraseology of our five notes, and shares with them only that it marks an exception to what the main text has just stated. Its opening v. 13 is not used in Jud. 1, is uncertain textually, and resembles elements of the introduction to Jos. 21. At first sight it was drafted by the editor who added this Calebite qualification. However it may be that the original introduction to this insert was later rewritten.[70]

I. Conclusions and Appendices

The report of the final seven allotted territories (18:11–19:48) is followed by two conclusions (19:49a and 51), after the first of which is mention of a grant to Joshua himself (vv. 49b–50); and two appendices, describing the provision of cities of refuge and cities for the Levites (Jos. 20 and 21). The Greek text concludes the account of the Levitical cities with a recapitulation of 19:49–50, the first conclusion and the grant to Joshua (and also a note similar to the LXX 'plus' in 24:31 about Joshua's burial in his home town of the stone knives used at the circumcision at Gilgal).[71] This repetition suggests that the second conclusion was added after Jos. 21:1–42 was inserted.

We are fortunate that the source for this longer appendix is still available to us—in the shorter and less clearly organized parallel in 1 Chron. 6:39–66. Recognition of this permits us to isolate the contribution of the Joshua editor of this material in the additions he made as he reorganized his source, and especially in the opening passage (21:1–3).[72] Within Joshua, this passage has affinities with 14:6a; 15:13; 17:4–6; and 19:51; and within Numbers, with passages to be discussed in our next chapter. Some of the information in the shorter appendix on refuge can be shown to be drawn from Jos. 21. Jos. 20 in fact seems to mark the reconciliation of once separate traditions about 'cities for the killer to flee to' and 'cities of *mkḷṭ* ('refuge'?)'.[73]

It appears that the longer appendices can be disposed of more quickly than the shorter conclusions, to which we must now return. For if the text of the Greek recapitulation is to be trusted, and if it is a repetition of what its editor found in 19:49–50, then we have evidence that the text of 19:49–51 has undergone change in both MT and LXX. This independent testimony may help us to plot the difficult relationship between MT and LXX in these verses—and, even more important, allow us to recover the original conclusion to the account of the distribution of the land in the book of Joshua.

The MT in Jos. 19 offers *wyklw lnḥl-'t-h'rṣ* in 49a and *wyklw mḥlḳ 't-h'rṣ* in 51b, both signifying something completed. In both places, LXX has the identical *kai eporeuthēsan embateusai tēn gēn*—the opening verb clearly representing *wylkw* (metathesis has occurred in one direction or the other), while the following verb is not the usual equivalent for *nḥl* or *ḥlḳ*, and is in fact unique in Greek Joshua. The Greek plus in Jos. 21 opens 'and Joshua completed dividing the land'—apparently a rendering of *wykl yhws' mḥlḳ 't-h'rṣ*[74]—a perfect complement to the command in 13:7.[75] It may be that the reviser in the Massoretic tradition who eliminated the repetition from Jos. 21 compensated by adding a note very like its introduction[76] to the end of 19:51—and that this prompted in the Greek tradition a 'correcting' repetition of the opening of v. 49. How 19:49a (MT) was produced remains unclear; but a conclusion with a plural subject is not unnatural after the full development of 14:1–5 and the answering 19:51a, where the business of land distribution is a corporate affair.

We find the name of Joshua's town and burial place also in the largely parallel notes Jos. 24:28–31 and Jud. 2:6–9, one of which represented the original link between the story of Joshua and that of the Judges. The drafter of that note apparently did not expect his readers to be familiar with the name—he described it as lying 'north of Mt. Gaash'. If that note belonged to the same stratum as Jos. 13:1, 7 and what we now see to be the original 19:49a, then we may have evidence that the grant to Joshua (19:49b–50) was a later addition—the name is not further qualified, and is assumed to be known.

J. Results

This fresh review, sensitive to the evidence of the LXX, of some of the recurring problems of the second half of the book of Joshua permits the following conclusions:

(1) The principal narrative stratum of Joshua did offer an account of the distribution of the land. On this point Smend's view is to be preferred to Wüst's. The structure of this original draft of the material in the second half of Joshua was something as follows:

(a) The introductory command, together with a note about Moses' previous grant in Transjordan to Reuben and Gad—Joshua was old and advanced in age; and Yahweh said to him, 'You yourself are old and advanced in age, and much of the land remains to be possessed fully. Now divide this land for settlement. From the Jordan to the great sea at the setting of the sun you will make grant of it—it is the great sea that will be the frontier.' To Reuben and Gad Moses made a grant across the Jordan to the east. Moses, servant of Yahweh, granted them from Aroer which lies on the edge of the wadi Arnon. . . . Then Gilead and the territory of the Geshurites and Maacathites . . . (Jos. 13:1, 7–9*, 11*—with the LXX as point of departure in vv. 7–9).

(b) The description of the territories of the ten tribes west of the Jordan—more or less what we find in Jos. 15:1–12, 21–62; 16:5–9; 17:1*, 2*, 7–10; and in 18:11—19:48, without the seven 'lot' introductions.

(c) The conclusion—the original wording of 19:49a, which is preserved now only as repeated in the LXX 'plus' following 21:42, followed naturally by 21:43–45—And Joshua completed dividing the land by its frontiers. So Yahweh gave Israel all the land which he had sworn to give their fathers, and they possessed it fully and lived in it. And Yahweh gave them rest on every side. . . .

(2) Several smaller additions to this first draft were made in the course of time: (i) A series of more or less homogeneous supplements can be detected in 13:2–6, 13; 15:63; 16:10; 17:11–13; 19:47 (LXX). These modify the information given at those points in the parent text to which they are appended. It is significant that the last of them pays tribute to *Ephraimite* pressure on the coastal area allocated to Dan, while the later and dependent Jud. 1:35 mentions instead the house of Joseph. (ii) Other possibly early, but not necessarily associated additions are Jos. 13:14, giving a rationale for Levi's absence from the tribal reckoning; 13:15–28, offering as detailed information on Reuben and Gad as was available in the following chapters on the other ten tribes; 15:13*, 14–20[77] on Caleb; and 19:49b–50 on the grant of land made to Joshua himself.

(3) There were two aspects to the major reorganization of the material to produce its present shape. First the pattern of ten separate tribal territories was broken by bracketing Ephraim and Manasseh together as Joseph (16:1–4; 17:14–18). Then the idea of a two-stage process of distribution was expressed in the narrative of 18:(1?)2–10 and the seven new 'lot' introductions in 18:11; 19:1b, 10a, 17a, 24, 32a, 40.

(4) The thesis of a half-Manasseh in northern Transjordan (Bashan) resulted in the addition of topographical material in 13:29–31, with compensatory adjustments in 17:1–6 and elsewhere.[78]

(5) Two major appendices of new material were finally added: the first on cities for the Levites (Jos. 21:1–42) and the other on cities of refuge (Jos. 20). It is with their terminology that other briefer elements such as Jos. 14:1b–3, 4–5, 6a; 15:13*; 17:4–6; and 19:51 appear related.

The significance of these conclusions will be further probed after our analysis of the traditions of land distribution in the book of Numbers.

NOTES

1. Cf. above p. 20.
2. The two principal studies are 'Joshua: the Hebrew and Greek Texts', *VT Suppl.* 30 (1979) and 'Textual and Literary Studies in the Book of Joshua', *ZAW* 90 (1978). Further implications are drawn out in 'Judges 1 and History: a Reconsideration', *VT* 25 (1975); 'A Judaean Sanctuary of ʿAnat (Josh. 15:59)?', *Tel Aviv* 4 (1977); 'The "Levitical Cities": Texts and History', *ZAW* 91 (1979); 'Cities of Refuge in Israelite Tradition', *JSOT* 10 (1978).
3. Tribute must be paid here to S. Holmes' pioneering study *Joshua: the Hebrew and Greek Texts* (1914), in which the implications of textual criticism for literary study were quite clearly perceived. Also to Orlinsky's paper in *VT Suppl.* 17, 1969.
4. This renders the sub-title of Smend's 'Das Gesetz und die Völker', already mentioned above, p. 44.
5. The reason for his terminology will be made clear below.
6. Cf. above, p. 4.
7. Smend notes Ehrlich's aesthetic comment (*Randglossen* III) that a geographical discussion, however long, has absolutely no place in a divine speech!
8. *rḳ* and *m'd* may be among the hallmarks of this interpolator—even if the latter is not 'original' in 1:7 (it is lacking in LXX) it is still attested in the similar 23:6.
9. Perhaps neither term does justice to the activity of the ancient writer. His first and foremost concern was to transmit the tradition he inherited—possibly from different sources. Attempts to co-ordinate any different points of view were secondary and without prejudice to this over-riding objective.
10. 'These nations that remain' (23:4, 7, 12) play a major role: Joshua has assigned Israel their territory; Yahweh will drive them out before the Israelites who will occupy their land. The wording corresponds to and is related to that in 13:1, 6; while 23:6 has a close link with 1:7–8.
11. Cf. above, n. 32 on p. 17.
12. The second account of convening an assembly had vexed him less than it does us—and in any case the repetition of 13:1a in 23:1b demonstrates that he is less than scrupulous in such matters.
13. *Prophetie und Geschichte* (1972).
14. F. M. Cross, *Canaanite Myth and Hebrew Epic* (1973), pp. 272–289.
15. Reference to Wüst's study was made at the end of our preceding chapter. Jos. 13:1–7 is dealt with on pp. 222–227.
16. Wüst insists that 13:9–12 is, from the point of view of literary history, secondary to the following information in vv. 15ff.
17. For example Num. 13:30; 21:24, 35; 33:53; Deut. 1:8, 21; 11:31; Jos. 1:11; 12:1.
18. Wüst argues (p. 225, n. 697) that Deut. 3:8, 10a and 12, 13a draw from Jos. 13:9, 11 and 15ff.
19. Smend now prefers the label DtrH (*Entstehung*, p. 115).
20. S. Mittmann, *Deuteronomium 1:1–6:3, passim*; and Wüst, *op. cit.*, pp. 9–57, 77–79.
21. 'Textual and Literary Studies in the Book of Joshua', *ZAW* 90 (1978).
22. *op. cit.*, pp. 202–205.
23. This type of construction, with a demonstrative (independent of a substantive) followed by the relative marker, is not common in the Hebrew Bible: *'lh 'šr* is found in Num. 34:29; Jos. 13:32; 14:1; Zech. 1:10; 1 Chron. 6:16; *zh 'šr* in Deut. 14:12; Jer. 33:16; and *hw' 'šr* in Gen. 42:14; Ex. 16:23; Lev. 10:3; 2 Kings 9:36; Jer. 41:9; 1 Chron. 5:36. Its translation must await the discussion of *nḥl* in Chapter V (p. 79) below.

24. Jos. 13:33 is a MT 'plus', discussed in my article noted above (n. 21).
25. The city lists of Judah and Benjamin (15:21–62; 18:21–28) following the descriptions of their borders (15:1–12; 18:12–20) are hardly comparable.
26. Against Wüst. The formal introduction which LXX offers between vv. 14 and 15 in the MT is also discussed in the article in *ZAW* 90.
27. The affinities of Jos. 14:1b–5 are noted below in section I of this chapter.
28. In Jos. 21:20, 40.
29. In 1 Chron. 6:51.
30. The only possible exception to this is Jos. 17:14, 17. In v. 14 *gwrl* is used in parallel to *ḥbl* and in close association with *nḥlh*. However it will be noted in section F below that this passage may be one of the latest elements in the book.
31. LXX attests *bn-mnšh* after the second *mkyr* also, while in the introductory v. 29 it is without the MT's repetition of the tribal name.
32. What might have been expected in v. 1 after the formal introduction appears only in vv. 7ff.
33. 17:1 does not read easily at all. It may be that the text has been modified to take account of an alteration in the relative status of Machir and Manasseh. It comes as a surprise after the mention of the primogeniture of Machir within the introduction to what one expects will describe the territory adjacent to Ephraim's to be told in the end that he had been allotted territory east of the Jordan. It may be polemic between Machir and Manasseh (and not between either of them and Ephraim) that explains the assertion *ky-hw' bkwr ywsp* in 17:1.
34. Bashan is East-Manasseh's territory according to 22:7—see p. 58 below.
35. De Vaux (*Early History*, p. 585) holds all of vv. 7–9 to be additional.
36. Where even Reuben and Gad are absent from the LXX.
37. With the one exception that it does not attest *bny* in v. 34.
38. In this case the appositional *bny-r'wbn wbny gd* in the MT of v. 25 will represent a gloss prior to the supplementation of the chapter.
39. Except 20:8—but it is certainly late (see below, section I).
40. In the already noted article in *ZAW* 90.
41. An important discussion of the meaning of *nḥlh* has been offered by Gerleman —'Nutzrecht und Wohnrecht', *ZAW* 89 (1977).
42. Here, more precisely, 'the nine tribes and the half tribe *of Manasseh*'. Wüst's quite different account of MT and LXX in these verses appears in *Untersuchungen*, pp. 85–86.
43. Jos. 1:12; 4:12; 12:6; and 18:7.
44. *Geographical and Topographical Texts*, pp. 161–169.
45. *bny mnšh* in v. 7, like *bny mnšh hnwtrym* in v. 2, correspond to a likely original (*mṭh*) *bny mnšh*, as attested by LXX, in v. 1.
46. That summaries were adjusted to conform to the information as it came to stand in the text is evidenced in the different numerical totals offered in MT and LXX in Jos. 15:44, 51, 57, 62.
47. The note in 17:1 about the primogeniture of Manasseh is often adduced in this discussion. This may be appropriate, but we noticed above (n. 33) another possible function for this claim.
48. Holmes (*op. cit.*, p. 65) notes that the sentence reads better in the LXX, and that its shorter reading appears to enjoy independent Vulgate support. But before accepting an *easier* reading, it would be preferable to be able to offer an explanation for the MT 'expansion'. A trace of it may be the replacement of LXX's 'God' with 'Yahweh'.
49. I hope to offer in the near future a detailed study of these and other problems posed by the LXX of Joshua.
50. In *VT* 25 (1975).

51. The term 'narrative' may even be too dignified for this short aetiological piece whose clumsy drafting has led many commentators to state that it was composed in two stages: vv. 16–18 completed by vv. 14–15.
52. *op. cit.*, p. 233.
53. In *OTS* 15 (1969), pp. 1–144.
54. And this agreement is the more striking given that there are several other differences between MT and LXX in these introductions.
55. But only in the context of its construction, its service, and what happens in front of it or at its door.
56. Within the broadly Deuteronomic books, only in Deut. 31:14; Jos. 18:1; 19:51; 1 Sam. 2:22; and 1 Kings 8:4.
57. Three studies in recent years have drawn attention to the significance of land in P's theology, and especially in the key-verse, Gen. 1:28. That is in fact the only biblical verse in which the *qal* theme of the same verb *kbš* is found with *'rṣ* as its (implied) object. While Brueggemann (*ZAW* 84, 1972), who holds that P concluded with the death of Moses, does not relate this to our Joshua passages, this step is taken by Blenkinsopp (*CBQ* 38, 1976) and Lohfink (*VT Suppl.* 29, 1978): Blenkinsopp urges that the use of the same uncommon verb 'suggests that with the allotment of land the command given at creation to fill the earth and subdue it has now been fulfilled' (p. 290); while Lohfink describes the use of this verb in Gen. 1:28 and Jos. 18:1, and nowhere in between, as the literary bracket round the whole P-work (p. 220). See again below p. 87, n. 52 and p. 120, n. 38.
58. This passage, like 17:14–18 (cf. p. 69, n. 49), requires clarification in a new detailed study.
59. Ex. 16:28; Num. 14:11; Jer. 47:6; Hab. 1:2; Ps. 13:2, 3; 62:4; Job 18:2; 19:2.
60. Margolis (p. 342) claims that the LXX's *eklēronomēsan* (without object expressed) renders the whole Hebrew phrase.
61. Deut. 10:9; 12:12; 14:27, 29; 18:1.
62. Num. 18:20 states that it is *Aaron* who is to have no *ḥlḳ wnḥlh* within Israel save Yahweh.
63. In vv. 6, 33, 34–38 in MT and LXX; and in MT alone in vv. 2, 25, 29, 31.
64. Some of the problems of Jos. 13:7–8 have already been mentioned on p. 59 above.
65. Num. 22:1; 32:19, 32; 35:14; Jos. 13:32; 14:3; 17:5; 20:8.
66. On pp. 65–66.
67. In the already cited article in *VT* 25 (1975).
68. *hwryš* is used in 13:6 and 23:5, 9, 13 while *'d hywm hzh* is found in 23:8, 9.
69. This seems preferable to Smend's view that part of DtrN's contribution is the related Jud. 1.
70. In the uncharacteristically longer Greek text of 15:13, the verse is composed of two co-ordinate clauses each with the verb 'give'—it could be that this marks a secondary expansion of the passage with elements like those in Jos. 21:1–3. Certainly the conclusion of the verse as attested in the Greek—*wytn lw yhwš'*—follows *'l-py yhwh* (LXX *h'lhym*) better than MT's concluding *lyhwš'*: not only is this use of the preposition unique, but the sense is also odd—for Moses if anyone is the intended agent of the divine word.
71. Rofé has recently shown that 24:31 is the prior text—*Shnaton* (1977), p. 227.
72. For fuller discussion see 'The "Levitical Cities": Texts and History', *ZAW* 91 (1979).
73. For fuller discussion see 'Cities of Refuge in Israelite Tradition', *JSOT* 10 (1978).
74. Rofé, *op. cit.*, p. 226, offers *lḥlḳ*—but there are half a dozen biblical parallels

to the use of *mn-* after *klh* in Jos. 19:51.

75. And so hardly an addition 'of no importance' as Soggin has it (*Joshua*, p. 202).
76. In fact if Joshua's name had been written in abbreviated form the concluding *wyklw* . . . would have been virtually indistinguishable from *wykl y* . . .
77. Following the insertion, 15:20 is a recapitulation of v. 12b that originally concluded the description of Judah's borders.
78. The addition of the majority of Jos. 22 must precede this 4th stage.

CHAPTER V

THE DISTRIBUTION OF THE LAND IN NUMBERS

A. The Close of the Book of Numbers

It is hard to avoid the impression that an earlier draft of the Pentateuch had ended close to Num. 27. Num. 20:12 records the sentence passed on Moses and Aaron after the rebellion at Meribah. Num. 20:22–29 reports the immediate execution of sentence on Aaron. The delay in Moses' case is to allow him to see the promised land from a mountain further to the north (27:12–14). The added delay between this repetition of sentence and specification of location and the final execution (at the end of Deuteronomy) is intolerable, and apparently secondary, from a literary point of view. The problem is not just the presence of the book of Deuteronomy at the end of the Pentateuch. The final chapters of Numbers exhibit in microcosm the same strains as the end of the now-canonical Moses-story in macrocosm—strains which there resulted in the repetition and expansion of Num. 27:12–14 in Deut. 32:48–52.

The report in the previous chapter (Num. 26) on a census of the whole people appears to have a double function: (a) after the forty years in the desert it offers an up-to-date count, replacing the earlier one reported in Num. 1; (b) it provides a factual basis for the distribution to Israel of the promised land (vv. 52–56). The prediction of Moses' death is preceded in 27:1–11 by legislation on female inheritance, and followed (vv. 15–23) by the installation of Joshua as leader. There follow a definitive list of sacrifices (chapters 28–29), legislation on women's vows (30), and a midrashic story on war with the Midianites that leads to legislation on the conduct of war and the taking of booty (31).

It is with Num. 32 that we return to the theme of land, albeit not the promised land west of the Jordan: here the circumstances are explained that led a minority in Israel to seek to settle east of the river, and their territory is described. In Num. 33:1–49 the whole period of the desert-wanderings is summarized in the form of a lengthy itinerary. And then at some length various aspects of settlement in western Palestine are dealt with in 33:50–34:29. By the penultimate chapter of the book, the future settlement is presupposed. Cities are allotted to the Levites from the whole people (35:1–8), of which six are denominated cities of refuge (35:9–34)—and here it is stated explicitly that we are dealing with an institution belonging to both sides of the Jordan. The book ends with a clarification of the regulations on female inheritance enunciated in 27:1–11.

It is not just the report of Moses' death that is delayed at the end of Numbers. There is a gap too between first and subsequent mention of the distribution of the land. After Num. 26:52ff. our attention is not again directed to the land west of the Jordan until 33:50ff. And just as the former report followed the account of a census which served in part to round off the desert story, so too this fuller latter section is preceded by a summarizing itinerary. The section itself is apparently in four main parts: (a) the dangers of inadequate conquest are outlined in 33:50–56; (b) a description is offered in 34:1–12 of the borders of the territory to be distributed; (c) we are reminded in 34:13–15 that part of the people is already settled in Transjordan; (d) a commission is appointed to oversee the distribution (34:16–29). Although this four-fold structure is coherent, there is evidence of secondary material in at least three of its sections.

B. The Topic Introduced

Num. 26:52–56 too is not an original unity. Wüst's stratification of this and most of the other Numbers passages to be discussed is very sensitive; and it is only over the implications of the detailed study of each passage that we differ.

(1) The core of this passage is vv. 52–54, which opens with the almost standard 'and Yahweh spoke to Moses saying' (52). Verse 54 makes tribal size the criterion for size of territory, in a phrase which will recur twice in the book of Numbers: *lrb trbh nḥltw wlmʿṭ tmʿyṭ nḥltw* (33:54, cf. 35:8). And the opening 'to these' and closing 'according to the number of the names' of the intervening verse show that the connection of this criterion with the preceding census is far from fortuitous—especially as the latter phrase appeared fourteen times in Num. 1 in the report of the first census. The remainder of the verse, *tḥlḳ h'rṣ bnḥlh*, could be understood quite as well actively with Moses as subject as passively with the land as subject (as in MT and versions).

(2) Introduced by *'k-bgwrl*, v. 55 adds in a rather laboured way the principle of lot to this simple and appropriate criterion. Its concluding phrase—*lšmwt mṭwt-'btm ynḥlw*[1]—is a quite unique formulation. Indeed, on the evidence of passages such as Num. 1:16; 7:2; and Jos. 22:14, one is inclined to posit an 'original' *lnśy'y mṭwt* . . . , and align this note to what is said in 34:16ff.—a scribe may have repeated *šmwt* in error from the end of v. 53.

(3) Finally v. 56, introduced by the unique variant *ʿl-py hgwrl* for *bgwrl*, attempts to make sense of the two principles—'It is by lot that its settlement will be divided (a distinction being made) between great and small.'

C. A Warning

The basis of the introductory formula in 33:50–51a—*wydbr yhwh 'l-mšh . . . l'mr dbr 'l-bny yśr'l w'mrt 'lhm*—is very common in broadly 'Priestly' strata of the Pentateuch. The intervening *b'rbt mw'b 'l-yrdn yrḥw* has particularly close parallels in Num. 26:3; 35:1.[2] Mention of the coming settlement (v. 51b) does follow this introduction elsewhere, but always in the words *ky tb'w 'l-h'rṣ.*[3] The participial construction which *ky* introduces here and in the almost identical 35:10—*'tm 'brym 't-hyrdn 'l-'rṣ kn'n*—has instead Deuteronomic affinities.[4] In almost every case it is found in a relative clause describing the land which the people are crossing to. In Deut. 4:22; 11:31; the phrase is prefaced by *ky*; and both contexts make an emphatic reading of the particle very suitable. Yet in Deut. 18:9, where our phrase appears in the singular, it is harder to decide whether *ky* is emphatic or means 'when'; accordingly, given the mixture of Priestly and Deuteronomic formulae in v. 51, it is hard to pronounce on the syntax of this participial phrase.

A blend of Deuteronomic and Priestly affinities characterizes the section as a whole. The verb *hwryš* appears most frequently in Deuteronomy, Joshua, and Judges—and in clearly related parts of Numbers and Kings/Chronicles. Linked in v. 52 with the following *w'bdtm* (pi'el) it is most reminiscent of Deut. 9:3 where it is followed by *wh'bdtm* (hiph'il). There are no close parallels to the rest of the language in v. 52: the nouns with suffix *mśkywtm* and *msktm* are unique;[5] and *hšmyd* is linked with *bmwt* only in Lev. 26:30, where God threatens to destroy the sanctuaries of a future rebellious Israel.

The repetition at the beginning of v. 53 of v. 52's opening *whwrštm* is striking, particularly in view of the changed object: simply *'t-h'rṣ* for *'t-kl-yšby h'rṣ*[6]—the object of *hwryš* is virtually always explicitly human.[7] It could be argued that *h'rṣ* is acceptable here as an abbreviation of the phrase in the previous verse; but it remains striking. The immediately following *wyšbtm-bh* has a precise parallel only in Deut. 11:31, where it follows *wyrštm 'th* (the qal verb regularly has *h'rṣ* or equivalent as its object—and *yrš* and *yšb* appear together in Deut. 17:14 and 26:1). Then the following *ky lkm ntty 't-h'rṣ* represents a common enough sentiment, but has no precise linguistic parallel; while the concluding *lršt 'th* is found only in Lev. 20:24[8]—common Deuteronomic usage is *lršth*.

The verbal theme *htnḥl* that opens the next verse has 'the land' as its object only in Num. 33:54; 34:13; and Ez. 47:13;[9] and is linked with *bgwrl* only in the Numbers passages. Within the settlement traditions, the only other occurrence of the verb is in Num. 32:18, a chapter whose literary stratification is notoriously complex. There its object is *'t-nḥltw*, also an element in 33:54—which makes one suspect that 32:18 is a reminiscence of the whole of 33:54. *htnḥl* appears elsewhere only in Lev. 25:46 and Is. 14:2, of possessing aliens as slaves. The following *lmšpḥtykm* in our verse is a form found precisely only in Ex. 12:21, while its answering *lmṭwt 'btykm* later in the verse is quite unique. At first sight neither form is remarkable; yet it is with a third person suffix that the former is very familiar, and even *'btm* is construed with *mṭwt* (as opposed to the regular *byt*) only in Num. 1:16 and 26:55. The statement of the principle of land-holding proportional to tribal size is probably derived from the almost identical 26:54—there without *'t* before the two occurrences of the object *nḥltw*, and with the first verb singular (*trbh*) like the second.[10] The following phrase—*'l 'šr-yṣ' lw šmh hgwrl lw yhyh*—is again quite unique, whether one follows the MT or accepts the testimony of the LXX that an original *šmh šm* has been shortened by haplography.

The phrase in v. 55 about leaving something over—*'šr twtyrw mhm*—is uncommon, but attested in three further contexts: Passover-food (Ex. 12:10; Lev. 22:30); manna (Ex. 16:19); and chariots (2 Sam. 8:4 = 1 Chron. 18:4). The noun *śkym* is unknown and the following *ṣnnym* occurs only in Jos. 23:13. There it is followed by *b'ynykm* which follows *śkym* here; here it is construed with *bṣdykm* which there follows a trio of nouns (*pḥ*, *mwqš*, and *šṭṭ*). Some link between these verses must exist. The following verb *ṣrrw* is used principally in the Psalms, but is found twice in Numbers (10:9 and 25:17, 18). Finally, there is no clear linguistic reminiscence of v. 56 anywhere in the Hebrew Bible; but the verse articulates the principle implicit in passages like Lev. 26:14–45 already quoted: that the fate Yahweh had in mind for the indigenous population of Canaan would be Israel's if she did not obey him.

The blend of Deuteronomic and Priestly terminology characterizes the whole of Num. 33:50–56: the blend is sufficiently striking for us to assert that it was drafted by someone familiar with both—but not in one piece. Most of the passage is an appeal to take the land fully—v. 54, with its precise prescription of the manner in which the land once fully taken will be allotted, constitutes an intrusion. As for the content of this insertion, it spells out more clearly than 26:56 how the apparently conflicting principles of division in 26:52–54 and 26:55 might be held together: that different sizes of territory be available for different sizes of tribe, and that the allocation of each to its own be effected by lot.[11] Perhaps v. 53, opening with *whwrštm* like v. 52 (but in a different sense because of the changed object) already begins the insert into the passage as first drafted.[12]

D. Israel's Borders

While 34:1 uses the completely regular form of the divine address to Moses, 34:2a has few close parallels. The imperative *ṣw* ('order') for the usual *dbr* ('speak') is used also in Lev. 24:2; and Num. 5:2; 28:2; 35:2—but only in Num. 28:2 do we also find *w'mrt 'lhm* that regularly separates the imperative from the content of the command. Then the participial phrase *ky-'tm b'ym 'l-h'rṣ kn'n* has a parallel only in Deut. 18:9—*ky 'th b' 'l-h'rṣ 'šr* . . .—if this were its model, it would be easier to explain the ungrammatical conclusion to the end of v. 2a in the MT; the Samaritan text has no definite article with 'land', but the more difficult MT may retain the evidence that *kn'n* represents an addition from the end of the verse.

The first part of 2b, *z't h'rṣ 'šr tpl lkm bnḥlh*, has a striking parallel in the introduction to Ezekiel's description of the land (47:14)—*wnplh h'rṣ hz't lkm bnḥlh*.[13] Then *lgbltyh* that concludes this verse and v. 12 is used also in Jos. 18:20 and 19:49; while *sbyb* that follows it in v. 12 has a close parallel only in Jos. 15:12 and 18:20.

The area defined in the main body of this section (3–12a) is almost if not exactly that implied in Jos. 13–19 and stated in Ez. 47:15–20 (there rather more briefly). Within Joshua there is a basis for detailed comparison and contrast only in the matter of the southern border—compare Num.

34:3–5 with Jos. 15:1–4. The borders in the west, and east except in the north, are capable of summary description: the Mediterranean sea, and the valley of the Dead Sea and Jordan. The *points* that mark the southern border in Joshua and Numbers are virtually identical. The exceptions are two: the names given separately in Jos. 15:3 as *ḥṣrwn* and *'dr* are found combined in Num. 34:4 as *ḥṣr-'dr*; and Joshua's following *hkrḳ'h* is additional to the names in Numbers. These differences together with the different *presentation* of the line in the two connecting texts makes very likely that neither text depends on the other, but both on a common list of names. Ezekiel's southern line is much more briefly stated. By contrast, Ez. 47:15b–17 offers a fuller description of the northern limits than Num. 34:7–9. However the integrity of both texts is unhappily in some doubt; and while it appears that they describe much the same line, there can be no certainty about literary priority.

The scanty results of this survey are the following: (1) The introductory vv. 1–2a of Num. 34 are an even more singular mix of Deuteronomic and Priestly language than 33:50–51. (2) The outer structure of the main body of the text (2b, 12b) has links with scattered elements of the territorial descriptions in Joshua, but more strikingly with the introduction to Ezekiel's account of the borders of the land. (3) The *details* of the actual frontiers are more similar to those in Joshua and Ezekiel than their presentation in the several texts now suggests. Some of the evidence (for example, combination or mis-division of names on the southern border) suggests as the common source a simple list of place names. Yet in Joshua some of the differences between MT and LXX are over the 'linking' vocabulary; and this may point to the practice of continuing elaboration and 'rectification' of the details of border accounts even after these had been set in their present literary frameworks. If so, our texts may have influenced each other before any one of them achieved its present form.

E. Transjordan

The close of our opening survey above talked of 33:50–34:29 as a coherent four-section passage as it stands. However it has to be recognized at the beginning of our discussion of 34:13–15 that it is the only one of the four sections not to start with the standard statement of Yahweh to Moses. Instead, it is introduced by a command of Moses to the people—*wyṣw mšh 't-bny yśr'l l'mr*. Then this section is the least independent of the four in content: its main function is to remind us why a list of only ten tribal representatives will suffice. And in fact the following vv. 16–29 could be conceived without it—Num. 32 is recent enough for the reader to be still familiar with the Transjordanian situation.

Then in a number of respects these verses are very clumsily drafted:

(1) The two relative clauses in 13b are difficult—

> 'this is the land which *you* will settle by lot
> which *Yahweh* has commanded be granted the 9½ *tribes*'.

The first follows naturally from the introduction in 13a, addressing the people of Israel in the second person. The second speaks in the third person of Yahweh commanding and nine and a half tribes being granted.

(2) Two oddities in vv. 14–15 are best explained as resulting from supplementation of the text. *lbyt 'btm* is used in 14 only after Reuben and Gad, but not half-Manasseh. And the opening verb *lkḥw* ('have taken') in the same verse is left hanging without its object till the end of the sentence when it is resumed before *nḥltm*—then *lkḥw nḥltm* is repeated in the summarising v. 15. In fact half-Manasseh is best seen as a supplement to v. 14—it is the extra delay to the object so caused that necessitates the repetition of the opening verb. Then at least the first part of v. 15 ('the two tribes and the half tribe have taken their settlements') will be a resumption of the expanded v. 14. (It is harder to decide whether or not the concluding 'across the Jordan east of Jericho' originally followed v. 14 or was drafted with the rest of v. 15.)

It appears then that an earlier draft of our passage read, 'And Moses commanded the people of Israel in these terms: "This is the land which you will settle by lot. For the tribe of the people of the Reubenites, according to their fathers' houses, and the tribe of the people of the Gadites, according to their fathers' houses, have taken their settlements (across the Jordan east of Jericho)."'[14] And this conclusion is in perfect harmony with one of the results of our preceding chapter, and with the literary situation in Num. 32.

That other mention of the half tribe in the book of Numbers is sudden and surprising. Our earlier discussions of that chapter have noted that it begins (vv. 1–32) as an account of dealings by Reuben and Gad with Moses—an account that is itself very probably the result of complex development.[15] At no point are we prepared for the talk in v. 33 about a grant of land by Moses to half-Manasseh as well as the other two tribes. And this talk becomes doubly suspect when we recognize that the description of that half tribe's land in vv. 39–42 is of a different type from that on Gad and Reuben[16] in vv. 34–38. The conclusion is unavoidable that talk of half-Manasseh in Num. 32 is supplementary to an already supplemented narrative.

However our suggested earlier draft of 34:13–15, if acceptable, may have a further implication. It becomes more natural to read the original part of the opening v. 13 as a new tailpiece to vv. 1–12: (1) Its talk of Moses commanding the people follows naturally from v. 2, which it resumes. (2) Its unusual hithpa'el verb *ttnḥlw* is a suitable resumption of *tpl lkm bnḥlh* in the same verse. (3) And it is likely that the specific *function* of v. 13 over against v. 2 is to assert that the land will be acquired by lot (*bgwrl*). This principle has already been enunciated in 26:55 and 33:54—but we have argued that both are additions to their contexts. However, if this is the original rationale of the first draft of v. 13, then the kernel of the remainder in v. 14 (and 15?) offers but a brief reminder of one of the results of Num. 32—and need not have been drafted with v. 13. The four sections of 33:50–34:29 as they stand may be coherent. But the third of them is secondary, and quite unnecessary until the principle of lot had to be written in. The themes of lot and half-Manasseh were once absent from the end of Numbers, as from the second half of Joshua.[17]

F. The Land Commission

The final section of our passage is introduced only by a report of the divine address to Moses (v. 16). The remainder details the content of this address in the form of a list, but does not, as in the first two sections, require that it be imparted to the people.[18]

It is most probable that here too we have material additional to the first draft. The opening words of vv. 17 and 19 are identical—*'lh šmwt h'nšym*; that already puts the reader on the alert that vv. 17b–19a are an insert. And the clumsiness of *tkḥw lnḥl 't-h'rṣ* in 18b after the matter-of-fact relative clause *'šr-ynḥlw lkm 't-h'rṣ* in 17b confirms that the two national figures, Eleazar and Joshua, have been added to the original commission of tribal leaders.

The main list has some formal irregularities:

(1) In the MT most tribes are styled 'tribe of the sons of . . .' (as in *mṭh bny šm'wn*) except for the first (Judah) and third (Benjamin). The reason in the case of *bnymn* could be simple haplography. However it must be noted that the LXX attests *bny* only before four of the ten names—Manasseh, Ephraim, Issachar, and Asher—and the first two of these could have been influenced by the immediately preceding and bracketting *bny ywsp*.

(2) In the MT—this time supported by both LXX and Samaritan—*nśy'* is found before the final seven names, but not the first three. That each tribe is to be represented by a 'leader' is stated in v. 18a, part of the insert into the original introduction. It is striking that the Syriac lacks a rendering of *nśy'* throughout the list of ten representatives; and this fact, taken with our literary conclusions, suggests that 'leader' was only secondarily added before the names from Dan to Naphtali in the tradition now represented by MT, LXX, and Sam.[19]

Aside from these formal irregularities, two aspects of the content of the original list call for immediate comment. The first is that the names of the representatives are unfamiliar, with the striking exception of Caleb from the tribe of Judah. And the second is that the order in which the tribes appear is not exactly parallelled in any biblical text, although it has close affinities with both Jos. 15–19 and Jud. 1: (a) All open with Judah, and Num. 34 and Jud. 1 continue with Simeon. (b) All have Manasseh and Ephraim in the middle.[20] (c) All present the four northern tribes together and in the same order—Zebulun, Issachar, Asher, Naphtali.[21]

Finally one detail of the outer structure of this section requires discussion. With the exception of Num. 32:19,[22] it is in v. 17a and v. 29 that we meet verbal forms of *nḥl* for the first time—excluding of course verses already shown to be secondary. The MT treats the first as the qal theme of the verb, with 'the land' as its object; and the second as a pi'el, with 'the people of Israel' as its object. And a similar interpretation is offered by the LXX which uses different Greek verbs. However the Syriac has read both as pi'el; and some Samaritan MSS make plain their causative reading of the form in v. 17 too by offering the hiph'il *ynḥylw* for *ynḥlw*. And this has led both editors of the text and commentators to argue, against MT and LXX, for a pi'el reading in v. 17.

The pi'el of *nḥl* is used in only three other texts in the MT—Jos. 13:32; 14:1; 19:51. In Jos. 14:1b its object is personal, as in Num. 34:29; whereas in Jos. 19:51 (*hnḥlt*) it is the areas taken into settlement/possession. Given such a choice, the briefer *'lh 'šr nḥl mšh* . . . of 13:32 is ambiguous—and of course this is quite as true of the answering kernel of 14:1–5, *w'lh 'šr-nḥlw bny-yśr'l b'rṣ kn'n*. It may be instructive to note that the verb *nḥl* in the qal theme has *nḥlh* as its object in Num. 18:23, 24; 35:8; Deut. 19:14; Jos. 17:6; and *'rṣ* in Ex. 23:30; 32:13; Jos. 19:49; Is. 57:13; Ez. 47:14. However *hnḥlt* of Jos. 19:51 with the pi'el is quite exceptional. Perhaps there is a better case for reading the verb there as qal, than for altering the form in Num. 34:17 to the pi'el.[23]

G. Levites and Refuge

If we consider Num. 35 on its own merits, we naturally deduce that it has grown by progressive supplementation. The provision of forty-eight cities for the Levites is first described (1–8); then six of these are defined as refuge cities (9–15); and finally the use and misuse of these cities is discussed (16–34). Only the mention of the six refuge cities in v. 6 within the first section appears to disturb this analysis—yet that verse is almost certainly intrusive: its heaviness in its context attracts attention, and it has apparently been designed (its opening words drafted on the basis of the first words of v. 7 or v. 8) to prepare us for the following section.

As to the formal structure of this chapter, it is in only two parts. Verse 1 is identical to 33:50, although the following imperative in v. 2 is *ṣw*, not *dbr*.[24] Then vv. 9–10a present the standard 'Priestly' introductory formula, followed in v. 10b by a repetition of 33:51b—exactly so in Sam., although MT offers *'rṣh* for *'l-h'rṣ*. (Verses 16ff. are clearly an expansion of vv. 9–15, rather than a new start.)

Num. 35:1–5, 7–8 expresses exactly the same conception of cities for the Levites as does Jos. 21.[25] In principle, it could either be derived from it or have served as part of its inspiration. That they represent fundamentally the same tradition is quite clear from the language they share: in both, the grant (a) is of *'rym lšbt* ('cities to live in'), (b) is made *llwym* ('to the Levites'),[26] and (c) comes from *'ḥzt bny yśr'l* ('the land at the people of Israel's disposal'). Then several of the expressions in Num. 35:1ff., while clearly related to those in Jos. 21, are fuller. The grant is also described as being made *mnḥlt 'ḥztm* and not simply *mnḥltm*. The associated 'pasture-lands' are *lbhmtm wlrkšm wlkl ḥytm* and not simply *lbhmtnw*. And then Num. 35:7 expresses the total more fully than Jos. 21:41. The fuller ones are more likely to be the derived forms;[27] and on these grounds we may agree with Noth's conclusion that Num. 35:1–8 does depend on Jos. 21.

There are links too between the actual content of the section on refuge in Num. 35:11–15 and Jos. 20. Although their opening commands are differently stated—*whḳrytm lkm* (Num. 35:11) and *tnw lkm* (Jos. 20:3)—the rare verb in Numbers was almost certainly used later in Jos. 20 in the first draft of v. 7.[28] Then vv. 11b–12 of Num. 35 are virtually identical to Jos. 20:3 (LXX). *mʿbr lyrdn* of v. 14 is again paralleled exactly in the LXX of Jos. 20:8. And there is a close, although not exact correspondence between the concluding Num. 35:15 and Jos. 20:9a.[29]

These brief observations document the interconnectedness of Num. 35:1–15 and Jos. 20–21. In Numbers as in Joshua, the material on the Levitical cities was composed before and without knowledge of that on the cities of refuge. And at least on this topic there are good grounds for considering the material in Joshua prior to that in Numbers. It is harder to plot the relationship between the passages on refuge. It is striking that the formal heading in Jos. 20:1–2a is unique in Joshua but common in Leviticus and Numbers.[30] At least some influence from these books (even if not from Num. 35:9–15) must be recognized on the drafting of our chapter in Joshua. And it may be that the combination which both passages exhibit of the concept of *mḳlṭ* and of cities to which a killer might flee was only achieved after more than one draft of both Jos. 20 and Num. 35:9–15.[31]

H. Numbers and the Distribution of the Land

Our first conclusion is simply stated. The brief introduction to our topic in Num. 26 (and originally only in vv. 52–54) is not only distant from the extended treatment in Num. 32–35, but also distinctive: (a) Its keyword is the only occurrence of any form of the verb *ḥlḳ* ('divide') in the book of Numbers. (b) Its principle of proportional allocation is repeated only in later elements within the final chapters.

Equally briefly stated is the admission that no new fundamental analysis of Num. 32 has been offered.[32] Some of the main features and difficulties of this notorious chapter have been noted. Yet comparative material is not as available for it as for most of the other texts treated in this study, which is attempting to secure a few reasonably assured results. It is to be hoped that some of these results (especially any relating to the language of Num. 32) may contribute to a reliable stratification of the narrative.

Num. 33:50–35:34 demands review in somewhat greater detail:

(1) Num. 35 represents a new beginning within this material. This is suggested by the repetition in v. 1 of the full formal introduction—including 'in the plains of Moab, near the Jordan opposite Jericho'—found

in 33:50, but not in the following 34:1, 16. And it appears confirmed by the remodelling in v. 8 of the proportional principle as stated with plural verbs in 33:54—one of the additions to the preceding unit.[33]

(2) The implications of this result for a discussion of the unity of 33:50–34:29 (shorn of its accretions) are harder to draw. We have established that the second section of Num. 35 was drafted after the first, and entailed its modification (v. 6). Was something similar true of the three sections of the previous passage? That it was (at least later) conceived to be one passage seems implied in the decision of the author of 35:1ff. to borrow its introduction for his new start, rather than to draft (under the usual briefer heading) what could be read as a new subsection. The structure of the kernel of 33:50–34:29 as a three-section passage is without difficulties; and the evidence concerning the unity of its material appears to be as follows:

(a) Both heading and contents in 33:50–52 (3), 55–56 represent a blend of broadly Deuteronomic and Priestly language and thought. And this is also true of the outer heading of the second section—34:1–2a.

(b) The immediate introduction to the description of the land (34:2b) is very similar to that in Ez. 47:14, including the rare phrase *npl bnḥlh*. With the verb in the causative hiph'il theme, we find the expression also in Jos. 13:6; 23:4;[34] and Ez. 45:1. Both forms of this expression belong to later strata in their respective books, and even if not interdependent will attest a similar (post-)exilic date.

(c) The description of the land itself is much harder to date. de Vaux has offered an attractive argument that Ez. 47's parallel account of the northern frontier reflects Assyrian province titles of the later eighth century, so that the basic points on the line shared with Num. 34 are earlier. Even if his argument holds, it does not date Ez. 47:15b–17 in its present state, although it may point to a quite early date for the geographical concept it embodies.[35] The one striking term in the present text of Num. 34:3–12a is the verb *tt'w* in vv. 7, 8, which is perhaps to be related to *wht'wytm* in v. 10. This verb has not been reflected in the territorial descriptions of Joshua or Ezekiel, and may have been unknown to and later than them both.

(d) As for the list of tribal leaders, the close similarity of tribal order with Jos. 15–19 and Jud. 1 (which is dependent on it) has been noted. And the use of the verb *nḥl* (even in the qal), while known in possibly earlier Pentateuchal contexts (Ex. 23:30; 32:13), is restricted in Joshua to later verses: 16:4; 17:6; 19:9, 49. Furthermore, its otherwise unique construction in 34:17 with *lkm* referring to those thereby advantaged *may* have a parallel in Jos. 19:51. There *lmṭwt bny yśr'l* could have a similar function after *nḥlw* read as qal, instead of being understood genitivally after *r'šy h'bwt*.

(e) One aspect of the list which warrants separate and more detailed scrutiny is the presence of Caleb (34:19) as Judah's representative. Part of the Biblical tradition makes it quite clear that the tribe of Kenaz to which he belonged was Edomite and descended from Esau.[36] In fact what most references to Caleb stress is not his affinity to this or that tribe, but his extraordinary faithfulness to Yahweh. The earlier passage that notes the special grant to him of Hebron (Jos. 15:13–19) is consistent with this view, and holds the allocation to be an exception to Judah's overall control of the south—and the note in Jos. 21:12 (=1 Chron. 6:41) marks an accommodation to this. Caleb is not viewed there as a special Judaean. Admittedly in the closely related but dependent Jos. 14:6–15 and Jud. 1:10–15 Caleb is 'Judahised' by implication or association.[37] And something similar seems to have occurred in 1 Chronicles, where towards the end of the long section on Judah in chapters 2–4 there is a brief Kenizzite genealogy in 4:13ff. Mention of Caleb in our text as representing Judah will belong to this later stage in the Caleb tradition. It is paralleled in Num. 13:6, where he is the Judaean among the twelve spies—although there is good ground to suppose that the list in 13:4–15 is even later than ours in Num. 34. We have accepted Wüst's argument that Joshua was originally absent from Num. 34—his tribe, Ephraim, is represented by the unknown Kemuel. Apart from Caleb, the other familiar name in Num. 13 is Hoshea (*hwšʿ* for the regular *yhwšʿ*) son of Nun appearing for Ephraim. Had our list been inspired in any detail by that in Num. 13, Joshua like Caleb would have appeared in its first draft.[38] The result of this five-fold summary of the evidence must be that nothing impedes the theory that Num. 33:50–34:29, stripped of its most obvious supplements, represents a broadly unified composition. It has drawn on relatively late elements in Leviticus/Numbers and in Deuteronomy/Joshua; and it has links with the final section of Ezekiel.[39]

(3) It remains only to point to the affiliations of the secondary elements within 33:50–34:29.

(a) Num. 33:54 and 34:13 are the only Biblical texts which construe the distinctive hithpa'el of *nḥl*[40] with *bgwrl*—and in fact *bgwrl* is linked with a form of the verb *nḥl* elsewhere only in the late Joshua texts 14:2(LXX); 19:51. The first draft of the supplementary 34:13 may have been devised to stress *bgwrl*. Even if this is true, it does not entail viewing it as prior to 33:54—the stress may be sufficiently explained by Moses having to explain to the people what to them was a novel idea. Num. 33:54 is of course later than 26:54—its model for the principle of proportional allocation; and its concluding *lmṭwt 'btykm ttnḥlw* is at least reminiscent of 26:55's difficult *lšmwt mṭwt-'btm ynḥlw*.

(b) As for the first draft of 34:14, *mṭh bny* is much less common as a marker of a tribal name than either *mṭh* or *bny* on its own.[41] What is quite unique to this passage is the use of this prefix before patronymic forms such as *hr'wbny/hgdy*, forms familiar in different contexts from the prefix.[42] Then the capping *lbyt 'btm* is common in Numbers and Chronicles. The final phrase of the verse—*lkḥw nḥltm*—is paralleled only in Jos. 18:7 and 13:8(MT).

(c) The form of enumeration of the nine-and-a-half and two-and-a-half tribes in the later additions to 34:13–15 can be likened only to Jos. 14:2–3.

(d) As for 34:17b–19a, Eleazar and Joshua are also to be found at the head of a commission in Num. 32:28; Jos. 14:1b; 17:4; 19:51; 21:1. But it is only in Jos. 17:4 that their associates are described as *nśy'ym*, as are the ten 'leaders' associated with Phinehas in Jos. 22:14. A further link with that latter verse's *nśy' 'ḥd nśy' 'ḥd (lbyt 'b*[43]*) lkl mṭwt yśr'l* may be seen at the beginning of Num. 34:18—*nśy' 'ḥd nśy' 'ḥd mmṭh*.

I. Numbers and Joshua Compared

In our discussion of the distribution of the land according to both Joshua and Numbers, we have attempted to be scrupulous in analyzing each book on its own, in unravelling independently the literary stratification of each. Where links between individual passages have been noted, these either still await clarification or only confirm results already more or less established. Yet it has been hard to keep control of the procedure; for the implications of these two chapters are very interesting. Our two books *are* quite as closely linked as has long been thought, but *not* as Noth or Mowinckel—or Wüst—have described the link.

(1) The first mention of our theme in Num. 26:52–54 uses the key phrase of the introduction (Jos. 13:1, 7) to the narrative of land-distribution in the principal stratum of Joshua—*ḥlk bnḥlh*. And its theory of proportional allocation corresponds well to the varying sizes of tribal territories actually listed in Jos. 15–19.

(2) The links in Joshua with the *first* draft of Num. 33:50–34:29 (a passage which of course assumes at least a version of the preceding Num. 32) are within the *supplements* that 'correct' the principal Joshua account.[44]

(3) Both lot and half-Manasseh represent late developments within Numbers as within Joshua.

(4) The appendix in Num. 35:1–5, 7–8 on cities for the Levites is related to Jos. 21 as is Num. 26:52–54 to the main stratum of Jos. 13–19. It utilises its distinctive language; and states the theory on which the more extended treatment had appeared to operate.

(5) The brief later elements within Num. 33:50–34:29 are linked in part with Num. 35:1–8, and also with those late supplements within Jos. 14–19 which share terminology with Jos. 21.

(6) The final major additions—Num. 35:9–15 and Jos. 20—on cities for refuge have also very close links.

J. Results

The interrelationships between the shorter insertions and the material on refuge detailed in (5) and (6) above require still closer scrutiny. And the very brevity of the former will make established conclusions the harder to achieve.

Grounds have been given, and more could be offered, for the priority of Joshua over Numbers in the case of almost all the material in question—in fact everything listed under (1) to (4) above).

The nature of Joshua's succession to Moses and the relationship between the two figures is differently portrayed in Num. 27:15ff. and parts of Deut. 34 on the one hand, and in Deut. 31 and Jos. 1 on the other. In the latter, Joshua simply takes over from Moses where he leaves off—and at Yahweh's command. But in the former, the very need for a successor is suggested by Moses (Num. 27:16–17), while Joshua's position is confirmed by Moses laying on hands (Num. 27:23; Deut. 34:9). To this corresponds Moses fore-ordaining in Numbers many of the details of the settlement and distribution of the land. Yet this canonical picture has been achieved only by the progressive supplementation of the traditions in Numbers on the basis of material in Joshua which itself was several times rewritten and reshaped. Most of that material is consistent with an estimate of Joshua as much more on a level with Moses.[45] And in fact it is only in the latest stages of the Joshua tradition that we find statements of Mosaic authority more familiar in Numbers—Jos. 14:2–5; 17:4; 21:2.

On a quite different tack, our general results permit us to sharpen an observation made above[46] about the order in which the ten western tribes are listed. If, like Jud. 1, Num. 34:19b–28 is *based* on Jos. 15–19, or an earlier draft of it, then we have even stronger evidence that (i) Manasseh was originally listed before Ephraim in Jos. 16–17, and (ii) Joseph is secondary.[47] Indeed we may deduce that Num. 34 preserves the original tribal order of Jos. 15–19 (Judah, Simeon, Benjamin, Dan, Manasseh, Ephraim, Zebulun, Issachar, Asher, Naphtali); and that Jud. 1 has relocated Dan at the end of the list in the far north, in deference to that book's more extended tradition on the Danite migration in chapters 17–18. To this result corresponds rather nicely the observation made above in chapter IV[48] that it is the territorial descriptions of the central and northern tribes only that employ the verb *pgʿ*. Different six-tribe federations prior to the canonical twelve-tribe Israel were reconstructed by Aharoni and Schunck on the basis of different readings of Jud. 1.[49] Our counter-claim might be at least that a separate source relating to Manasseh, Ephraim, Zebulun, Issachar, Asher, and Naphtali underlay the first draft of Jos. 15–19. Of the remaining four tribes, two of Judah's immediate neighbours —Simeon and Dan—are described in terms very like her own town lists; and town lists are also offered for Benjamin.[50] It may be that these new literary observations will permit a fresh appraisal of the history of the topographical source-material in Joshua.[51]

A final word. It is in this *normal* sense that it is appropriate to use the term 'source' in discussing the end of Numbers and the second half of Joshua. Our last chapter demonstrated that in Joshua we are dealing with geographical information presented, corrected, expanded, extended, fundamentally reshaped, and still further added to. Some of these alterations were indebted to sources of a similar order—the longest example being Jos. 21; while others represent nothing more than a denial that an assertion in the earlier draft was true, or completely so. And this chapter has shown how the final stages of the Mosaic tradition gradually appropriated this developing Joshua tradition. How our conclusions relate to what has traditionally been known as 'source-analysis' in the Pentateuch and Joshua must be more fully discussed in our next chapter.

Noth's instincts were correct (although many of the details of his arguments wrong) that the solutions to the problems of the end of Numbers lay in a new understanding of the book of Joshua. Mowinckel's attempt to claim for P of the Pentateuch both command in Numbers and fulfilment in Joshua was doubly unfortunate: it ignored the literary indebtedness of Numbers to Joshua; and it laid too much stress on passages like Jos. 14:1–5 and 19:51 which have proved to be occasional supplements, not evidence of major editorial activity.[52] Much of the detail in Wüst's fresh and fundamental study has proved of great help to the present one—especially in the book of Numbers. It may have been lack of attention (shared by too many other scholars) to the importance of the LXX of Joshua for that book's literary analysis that prevented similar success throughout. His conclusions about the inter-relations of our two books are consequently so much more complex than our own.

NOTES

1. The Samaritan tradition offers the hithpa'el *ytnḥlw*.
2. The other passages with *'l-yrdn yrḥw* are Num. 26:63; 31:12; 33:48; 36:13.
3. Lev. 23:10; 25:2; Num. 15:2.
4. Deut. 2:4; 4:14, 22, 26; 6:1; 11:8, 11, 31; 31:13; 32:47; Jos. 1:11.
5. Within the neighbouring books, *mśkyt* is found only in Lev. 26:1—and elsewhere only in Ez. 8:12; Ps. 73:7; Prov. 18:11; 25:11. As for *mskh*, it is found in apposition to *psl* and construed with both *'lhy* and *'gl* (cf. Deut. 9:12, 16), but never with *ṣlm(y)* as here.
6. One of several LXX variants in this passage is its repetition of the fuller object in v. 53; but the Hebrew is to be preferred.
7. The only certain exception is Jos. 17:12, where 'these cities' follows the verb —in Jos. 8:7, where it is construed in MT with 'the city', LXX attests a different verb.
8. Compare *lršt 'tw* in Jos. 24:4.
9. Perhaps for completeness we should include the Samaritan Num. 26:55, as noted above—although the object is not there expressed.
10. Both verbs are singular in Sam. and plural in LXX.
11. Unhappily it is easier to produce this form of words than to produce a method for giving effect to it.
12. Verse 53, like v. 51b, shares terminology with Deut. 11:31. This need not reflect the activity of the first drafter of the passage, but may derive from a later scholar who noted the link and built upon it.
13. The phrase *npl bnḥlh* is used also in Jud. 18:1 and Ez. 47:22—but in the one there is textual uncertainty, and in the other the form of the phrase is difficult.
14. The assumption appears to be that 'the people of Israel' are the ten remaining tribes—an assumption shared in 33:51 and 34:2.
15. Cf. our own discussion on pp. 15, 32 etc. above; and the new analyses by Mittmann (*op. cit.*, pp. 95–104) and Wüst (*op. cit.*, pp. 91–109).

16. The varying attestation of this order of the names has already been mentioned in chapter IV above, p. 70, n. 63.
17. The first part of this conclusion runs counter to Wüst's result. He argues that 34:13 (to the end of the first relative clause) was drafted along with the introduction to 34:1–12—and in fact represents the first statement of the principle of lot (*op. cit.*, pp. 192–3).
18. The people are referred to in the concluding v. 29 as the beneficiaries of the grant of land—and indeed this is probably anticipated by the plural *lkm* in v. 17a that will include the people with Moses.
19. Variation in the styling of individual tribes is common in other lists in Numbers, and so is unremarkable here.
20. It was noted above in chapter IV that the present order of the material in Jos. 16–17 may not be original.
21. Except that Jud. 1 nowhere mentions Issachar.
22. Num. 32 has not yet been reviewed in detail; however both Mittmann and Wüst (cf. above n. 15) see v. 19 as one of the later elements in the chapter.
23. See further p. 81 below. A causative reading of *nḥlw* certainly correlates well with the transitive *ḥlḳ* at the end of the verse; however v. 51b may be later than v. 51a and consequently irrelevant for its original interpretation.
24. For further references see section D above on 34:2a.
25. I mean those parts of Jos. 21 added by the editor who added the chapter to the book of Joshua. On this point, see further my article in *ZAW* 91.
26. As opposed to *lbny lwy*.
27. This may find corroboration in the suggestion that *nḥlt 'ḥztm* (Num. 35:2) represents a combination of *nḥltm* (Jos. 21:3) and *'ḥzt bny yśr'l* (21:41).
28. LXX's *diesteilen/an* certainly does not represent MT's *wyḳdšw*, which probably represents the assimilation of the unfamiliar *wyḳrw* to the following place name *ḳdš*.
29. Jos. 20:9b is virtually identical to the LXX 'plus' at the end of 20:3, which as has just been noted closely resembles the end of Num. 35:12.
30. With of course the one change that it uses Joshua in place of the familiar Moses.
31. Some of the possible indicators of disunity within Jos. 20 are the discrepancies between vv. 7 and 8 (the names in v. 7 are listed from north to south and are defined geographically; those in v. 8 from south to north and defined tribally) and the introduction in v. 9 of a new (and unique) technical term—*'ry hmw'dh*.
32. Cf. above nn. 15, 16 and 22.
33. It is possible to reverse this second argument—however the first is probably decisive on its own.
34. That Num. 33:55 is also linked with Jos. 23 has been observed above.
35. de Vaux, *Early History*, pp. 128–132. His arguments about the northern frontier are not discussed by Kallai in his recent paper cited in chapter III above—but he does refer there to a more detailed Hebrew article in *Eretz Israel*, vol. 12.
36. Cf. Gen. 36 and 1 Chron. 1.
37. It could be argued (although I am not persuaded) that the opening words of Jos. 14:6 about the approach of the men of Judah to Joshua at Gilgal were drafted separately from the following narrative and for the purpose of linking it to the book as a whole. However the clear implication of the whole verse as it stands is that Caleb addressed Joshua as one of the men of Judah. Then Jud. 1:10–15 opens by attributing to Judah initiatives taken in Joshua by Caleb—when the latter is finally mentioned in v. 12 he appears to be a Judaean.
38. The actual list in Num. 13 has long been regarded as later than its context P^s rather than P^g, in the traditional terminology. Beltz (*op. cit.*, pp. 11–18) argues

that several of the names show Persian influence. If this argument holds, it could just be that Num. 34 has had further influence on the drafting of Num. 13: 13:21 gives the extent of the mission of the spies as being *mmdbr-ṣn 'd-rḥb lb' ḥmt*; and while *lbw' ḥmt* appears in several other Biblical texts as a symbol of the land's northern extent, the only other text in which it is found with *mdbr-ṣn* is Num. 34:1–12.

39. In his large-scale commentary (pp. 1212–3) Zimmerli is non-committal as to whether the end of Ezekiel may be seen as a *terminus ad quem* or a *terminus a quo* for our Numbers material. Wüst (p. 32, n. 106) on the other hand argues that Ezekiel has transformed Num. 34:2b, 13 into an introductory address by Yahweh (47:13a, 14b) and consequently replaced the original introduction by a new one (15a).
40. Used only in Lev. 25:46; Num. (26:55—Sam.) 32:18; 33:54; 34:13; Is. 14:2; Ezek. 47:13.
41. And in the book of Joshua at least, where we have some text-critical control, we must often suspect that scribal expansiveness has been at work when we meet *mṭh bny*. For further discussion of tribal terminology, see my 'Joshua: the Hebrew and Greek Texts'.
42. In Deut. 3:12, 16; 4:43; 29:7; Jos. 1:12; 12:6; 13:8; 22:1; 2 Kings 10:33.
43. Not in the Syriac, and possibly a supplement.
44. Num. 33:55 with Jos. 23:13 and 34:2 with 13:6; 23:4.
45. The grant to him of a personal plot of land (Jos. 19:49–50) and the description of his death and the subsequent lapse into the period of the Judges (Jos. 24:28–31, cf. Jud. 2:6–9) both point to his personal prominence as one of the founding personalities.
46. In section F.
47. Joseph is in fact quite differently handled in Joshua and Judges 1. The assault of the house of Joseph on Bethel (Jud. 1:22–26) has no clear links with material elsewhere in Joshua or Judges; and no explicit connection is made between Joseph and the following Manasseh and Ephraim. Both points testify against any dependence on Jos. 16–17 as we know them.
48. Again in section F.
49. Cf. chapter III above, pp. 39–41.
50. In fact both Benjamin's border-description and her town lists are concluded by *z't nḥlt bny bnymn* (Jos. 18:20, 28). This is unlike the situation in Jos. 15 on Judah, where (a) the border-description closes with *zh gbwl* . . ., (b) *z't nḥlt* . . . in v. 20 is apparently a recapitulation of this phrase in v. 12b, and (c) the town-lists end in v. 62 without formal conclusion. This, taken along with Schunck's just cited observations, makes one at least ask whether Benjamin's border-description is not secondary to her town-lists.
51. That renewed attention to text-criticism permits a similar reappraisal I have attempted to show in my already cited paper in *Tel Aviv* 4.
52. Lohfink's discussion of these two verses (cf. above p. 70, n. 57) claims them for P on rather different criteria: (1) that they do *not* presuppose their present context in Joshua; but (2) that they are to be expected on the basis of the narrative system of P^g. For a final comment on this approach see below, p. 120, n. 38.

CHAPTER VI

JOSHUA AND THE PENTATEUCH

A. Introductory

Our discussion to this point has left some things unsaid. At the same time it has made it likely that there are some other things still to say. The concentration of the two preceding chapters on the theme of the land and its distribution in Numbers and Joshua may have opened new perspectives on the development of the relevant sections of these two books. We may have persuaded ourselves that it is not helpful to see the hand of the Pentateuchal 'Yahwist' in the series of corrective notes to the first draft of geographical information in the second half of Joshua—still less in the present introduction to the book of Judges which in part depends on them. But nowhere have we considered the equally long-standing claim that some of the material in the first half of Joshua is a continuation of the earlier strata of the Pentateuch. We may have succeeded in offering a relative stratification of Jos. 13–21. But nowhere has the similarity between the language and interests of the final strata and those of some 'Priestly' material in the Pentateuch been discussed. The unsaid needs now to be said.

On the other side, our results so far encourage us to take a few further steps—to confront some of the persistent questions of Pentateuchal scholarship. Chapter V confirmed the presence at the end of Numbers of both 'Priestly' and 'Deuteronomic' elements. Do the final chapters of that book represent the culmination of work on the Pentateuch, or do they only anticipate and render easier the addition of the book of Deuteronomy to the Moses traditions in Exodus-Numbers? The fact that we still possess their source material in Deuteronomy and (especially) Joshua enables us to plot some of the activity of the 'Priestly' editors of the end of Numbers. This situation is of course exceptional. That we can cross-check is unique. But is the conclusion of Numbers also *sui generis* to the extent that we are debarred from drawing conclusions about the preparedness of the 'Priestly' editors earlier in the Pentateuch to absorb material from other (now unknown) sources and present it as Mosaic legislation? What is still to be said must now be said.

B. Do earlier Pentateuchal strata continue in Joshua?

Confidence in discussion of the pre-Deuteronomistic material in Joshua, as of the 'JE' material in the Pentateuch, must inevitably be of a lesser order than is possible in the discussion of the work of the Deuteronomists themselves. Their own plan is more obvious, like the main architectural phase in an old building. Over what they inherited, what they found 'on the site', we can pretend to much less certainty. Even where sizeable traces remain, their originally intended functions and inter-relationships often remain quite elusive. Discussion of such matters must accordingly be briefer or more extended than in the case of other topics in this book—and here the former alternative is more appropriate. What follows is but a brief review of some of the more recent studies bearing on the matter—some already mentioned above in chapter III.[1]

(1) *Beltz, Caleb, and 'L'*

Beltz's monograph on the Caleb traditions[2] quite deliberately takes its starting-point from Eissfeldt's and others' analysis of the earlier Pentateuchal/Hexateuchal narrative into three parallel strands.[3] The kernel at least of the Caleb stories in Num. 13–14 and Jos. 14–15 shows that the Calebites are of military character and have an aggressive attitude towards the settled land. Then the genealogies in 1 Chron. 2 and 4 show that they maintained a very independent existence of semi-nomadic nature right into the post-exilic period. It is this tribe that was the social force lurking behind the source L. Accordingly the point of departure of L was not any sort of cultic tradition, but rather the attempt of a tribe to assert itself through its tribal history against a power seeking to usurp it ideologically—in fact the power of the kingdom of Judah and the temple of Jerusalem.

His argument has several attractions. His isolation of the distinctive 'moments' of the Calebite traditions is helpful, if not particularly novel. But what appears much more doubtful is whether the few Calebite texts provide a wide enough basis for making the claims Beltz does about L—even granted the Eissfeldt three-strand hypothesis. It is something of an embarrassment to him when discussing the L-material in the primeval history that Caleb is a Kenizzite and not a Kenite. That these two southern clans may have shared many traditions is thoroughly plausible[4]—but that the Calebite L-source was the vehicle by which Kenite tradition was introduced into the canonical Hexateuchal narrative demands demonstration. Again, that Jos. 14:6–15 and 15:13–19 reflect authentic tradition is thoroughly plausible; but that their links with the Calebite material in Num. 13–14 suffice to prove the presence in Joshua of a Pentateuchal narrative source, in any meaningful sense of these terms, is most questionable.

(2) *Langlamet, Rahab, and the Hexateuch*

Langlamet's paper on Jos. 2[5] opens with a succinct but detailed review of the debate over the Pentateuch in the previous century.[6] He rejoices in the apparent conservatism of the leading Old Testament Introductions. Without the conquest stories, the traditions of the Pentateuch are at least partially deprived of their meaning—and Noth would be the last to deny this. What is necessary, given the rapid oscillations of previous exegetical research into Joshua and the opening of Judges, is a search for sufficient convergent indicators to render the attribution of their strata to Pentateuchal sources practically certain. The resumé in the second section of his paper of the analyses of Jos. 2 by different scholars demonstrates the inadequacy of the presuppositions of the majority—the great exceptions being Smend, Eissfeldt, and Rudolph.

His most striking contribution is his tabulation of all biblical chapters that share more than five words or expressions with Jos. 2. These are to be found predominantly in the Pentateuch, but also throughout the Former Prophets. And the three chapters that head the table are Gen. 24, with 19 correspondences, Gen. 19 with 17, and Jos. 6 with 14. He finds the overlap established with Gen. 24 particularly striking in that (a) the atmosphere and themes of the stories of Abraham's servant and Rahab are so different, and (b) the contacts are disseminated throughout both chapters. Similarly, with Lot's entertainment of the messengers, the contacts are hard to explain on the basis of analogous situation. In Jos. 6 however, almost all the contacts with Jos. 2 are grouped in vv. 22, 23, 25; this makes Langlamet suspect the activity of a redactor forging links between Jos. 2 and 6—perhaps Noth's *Sammler*.

His conclusion is that Jos. 2 was part of the document J. Closely argued though it is, guarded though it is, this is heavily dependent on his confessed assumption that the Pentateuchal narratives lose part of their sense without those of Joshua to follow—a point where he is happy to cite Noth in his support. But Noth's own principal criterion for the attribution of any passage to one of the familiar sources—connection with the already familiar narrative—is not examined. He admits that affinities between Jos. 2 and other parts of the Former Prophets have much to do with the animation of popular bards whose language and narrative procedures were transmitted across the centuries. In no way do they prove the existence of a J story till Jehu. But no less, they do demonstrate the seriousness of the efforts that have been made to find as far as the book of Kings a stratum related to the Yahwist traditions.

The main conclusions of Langlamet's earlier monograph on the complexities of Jos. 3–4 have already been reviewed above in chapter III. Now, following this treatment of Jos. 2, he published a complementary note on the crossing of the Jordan and the documents of the Hexateuch to probe whether further answers to the problems of these chapters could be gained from this 'superseded' method.[7] Having listed the affinities of each word or phrase, he found to his delight that few retractions were necessary from his previous analysis—and in fact that the conclusions of his earlier study could now be linked with the most assured positions of classic literary criticism. Certainly a good illustration of what a quest for convergent indicators can produce. Yet again Noth's challenge is not explicitly taken up: to make narrative consistency the sole—or at least the main—criterion for the separation of strata.

(3) *Otto, Gilgal, and J*

Otto has sought to reconstruct the ritual of the ancient festival of unleavened bread at Gilgal on the basis of a traditio-historical examination of the two broadly parallel literary sources produced by his analysis of the text of Jos. 1–12.[8] It is only the primary literary-critical aspect of his study that concerns us here.[9]

He begins with the chapters where we have already noted the literary problems to be most acute. Supplementary hypotheses like those of Rudolph and Noth cope only inadequately with the numerous doublets in Jos. 3–4; and these chapters can be separated into two accounts, now combined with little alteration or addition to either. The one which serves as the basis had been composed or at least reworked by a Deuteronomist.

Otto has shown himself from the beginning to be aware that the LXX offers markedly different testimony to the text of Joshua from the MT; and he is indebted to the sensitive section on textual criticism in Langlamet's *Gilgal* monograph just discussed above. Yet oddly it is only as he turns to Jos. 6 that he sketches the (lesser) worth of the shorter LXX. Langlamet's and Otto's reservations about the LXX tradition in Joshua warrant far more detailed consideration than is possible here. Just two brief observations may be made. The first is that all the MT pluses in Jos. 3–4 which Langlamet deems 'original', while Holmes[10] prefers the briefer LXX, occur in one or another of Langlamet's three redactional phases—not in any of his narrative or catechetical sources.[11] Indeed Holmes' textual conclusions may support Langlamet's literary ones, for the MT's 'supplements' would be a form of redaction. The second is that of the few verses in Jos. 8:1–29 which Otto attributes to his 'Deuteronomistic' source, and which are necessary to bring its reader to its climactic altar-building in vv. 30–35, all but one half verse is lacking from the LXX—and even that v. 3a is unexceptionable in the context of the shorter Greek chapter. Most commentators would agree with Otto that Jos. 8:30–35 are no original part of their present context; but to link them to a main Deuteronomistic stratum of Joshua by means of a series of unacknowledged MT pluses appears irresponsible.

Otto's deduction that analysis into parallel sources is unnecessary in Jos. 1, most of which is Deuteronomistic,[12] or in Jos. 5; 7; 9–11; which are largely the contribution of his earlier source, shows his approach to be less novel than at first appears—at least as far as the reading of each separate chapter is concerned. Yet his arguments about the Deuteronomist in Jos. 8 have already been shown fragile; no less so is his claim that the bulk of Jos. 2–11 represent the conclusion of the Pentateuchal source J, on the twin grounds that it shares terminology with J of the Tetrateuch and that it makes a good conclusion to the story begun in Num. 32.[13]

(4) *Tengström and the Hexateuch-narrative*

Space again permits only a mention of some aspects of Tengström's 'literary-historical'[14] study of the Hexateuch shorn of its main legal sections.[15] He is content still to talk of a 'Hexateuch' because (a) the narrative of the Pentateuch is incomplete, and (b) we find influence of Deuteronomy in Genesis-Numbers and of P in Joshua—the topic of our own next section. And this despite lodging a complaint against traditional criticism for paying scant attention to the total conception of a work! Several convergent indicators suggest that the origins of the Hexateuch are not in early monarchical Jerusalem, but premonarchical Shechem and central Palestine; and Tengström's monograph offers a delineation of this basic composition which differs from most scholars' 'J' in two immediately striking ways: it includes material often assigned to 'E', such as Gen. 21 and 22; and it excludes the Sinai and Balaam complexes.

What concerns us most here is his handling of the book of Joshua. Like Otto he finds the most acute problems of literary analysis in chapters 3–4 and 6, although their solutions differ markedly. Unlike Otto he attributes most of Jos. 1 and the kernel of 8:30–35 to his basic composition of the Hexateuch, but not Jos. 5. Some critical decisions he finds complicated by the great importance of possession of the land in Deuteronomic theology. This had resulted in the pre-Deuteronomic account of the taking of the land proving a particularly significant source for the Deuteronomistic historians, which renders all the more difficult a separation of Deuteronomic from pre-Deuteronomic elements in the Joshua narrative.

No one will find fault with his labelling Jos. 1:7–9 Deuteronomistic—along with most of 8:30–35. But our earlier discussion of development, elaboration, and correction even *within* the Deuteronomistic milieu suggests that Tengström's conclusion is all too simple that Jos. 1:1b–3, 5–6, 10–18 and 8:30, 31b were part of his pre-Deuteronomistic basic composition. The fragility of such literary conclusions calls into question some of Tengström's comments about the structure of his proto-Hexateuch—in particular that the altar building which might have been expected to follow the revelation of the divine name in Ex. 3 is delayed until conditions are right: that is until Shechem is achieved in Jos. 8. It cannot be denied that there are echoes far from coincidental in Joshua of material in the Pentateuch: such as Joshua's leading his people to a choice for Yahweh, God of Israel, at Shechem (Jos. 24:24) and Jacob's erecting an altar at Shechem called El, God of Israel (Gen. 33:18–20). But that these are not merely echoes—although of course calling for analysis and explanation—

but also deliberate structural pivots of a literary composition is far from clear. We have already demonstrated that those responsible for drafting some of the end of Numbers desired to bring that book into line with traditions already recorded in Joshua. This is not in itself a ground for claiming that clear links were forged only in the *final* stages of the composition of the Pentateuch and Joshua. But it does mean that this kind of solution must be considered before others are too readily espoused.

(5) *Seidel and Jericho*

Seidel's paper on the collapse of Jericho—subtitled 'Exegesis without Kerygma?'—has at its centre a very different approach to the literary complexities of Jos. 6: representing an advance on Noth's method rather than an alternative route.[16] He posits a development towards the present text in five stages from a ritual beginning that had no link with the conquest story: (i) ritual (7 priests with wind instruments); (ii) cult legend of Jericho (procession—ram's horn signal—collapse of the walls); (iii) (a) editorial annotations (priests blow the trumpets) and (b) total reshaping on the pattern of an ark procession; (iv) Jericho conquest saga; (v) Deuteronomistic additions. Seidel sees it as not at all impossible that it was first at Gilgal that Jericho's collapse was celebrated ritually as part of a memorial of settlement and conquest. And in this he is close to Otto. Where he differs is in his emphasis that none of the layers of Jos. 6 is to be associated with any one or more of the sources of the Pentateuch (N, J, E or P).

If his analysis can be sustained, it seems to offer a better way forward than those just reviewed. The complete re-orientation of the original material (the second part of his third stage) persuades him that Noth's term *Sammler*—collector—is not quite appropriate. And he feels he has hit on a piece of priestly tradition which developed *before* P and which has hardly been noticed in discussion of the development of the Deuteronomists' work. And that comment may be sufficient reminder of our own next business.

C. Priestly Joshua?

At the end of chapter IV above it was noted that parts of the substantial appendices in Jos. 20 and 21 appeared related in language and interests to some briefer elements in the preceding chapters, such as 14:1b–3, 4–5, 6a; 15:13*; 17:4–6; and 19:51. It is these passages in Joshua that are most reminiscent of 'Priestly' material within the Pentateuch—and not just in the related final chapters of Numbers. Accordingly it must now be our business to probe these literary relations more closely.

A useful starting point may be to review where else in the Bible we find the language used by the editor of Jos. 21—or, more precisely, within those elements of Jos. 21 whose originality is confirmed by the LXX and which do not appear in its major source, viz. 1 Chron. 6:39–66:

(1) *wygšw . . . 'l . . . wydbrw/wy'mr(w)* is paralleled only in Num. 32:16; Jos. 14:6a.

(2) *r'šy 'bwt hlwym* we find only elsewhere in Ex. 6:25, while the similar and subsequent *r'šy 'bwt hmṭwt lbny yśr'l* in 21:1 occurs in Num. 32:28 and Jos. 14:1b—and, without *'bwt* in Num. 30:2. Then *r'šy 'bwt* is construed with *h'dh* in Num. 31:26. The similar expression *r'šy h'bwt l-* is found in Num. 36:1; Jos. 19:51; 1 Chron. 15:12; 24:6, 31; 26:21, 26; 2 Chron. 5:2; 19:8; 23:2; 26:12—and, without the definite article, in Num. 36:1; 1 Chron. 8:6; 9:9, 33.

(3) Eleazar the priest and Joshua son of Nun appear together in Num. 32:28; 34:17; and Jos. 14:1b; 17:4; and 19:51. (It is Moses who is paired with Eleazar in leading the chiefs of the congregation in Num. 31:13, 26, and 32:2.)

(4) The plural *mṭwt* (tribes) is construed with 'people of Israel' only in Num. 30:2; 32:28; 36:8, 9; Jos. 14:1b; 19:51; 21:1; and 1 Kings 8:1 (=2 Chron. 5:2)—and without 'people of' in Num. 31:4; Jos. 22:14.

(5) Shiloh is specified as being in the land of Canaan elsewhere only in Jos. 22:9 and Jud. 21:12.

(6) *yhwh ṣwh byd-mšh* occurs in Ex. 35:29; Lev. 8:36; Num. 15:23; 36:13; Jos. 14:2; 17:4 (LXX); Jud. 3:4.

(7) 'Cities to live in'—*'rym lšbt*—is a phrase used only in Num. 35:2 (and cf. v. 3); Jos. 14:4. It could be suggested by *mwšbwtm* in 1 Chron. 6:39a, the introduction to the source of Jos. 21.[17]

(8) The noun *mgrš* ('grazing land') occurs most often in plural forms. Outside Num. 35, Jos. 21, and 1 Chron. 6, these are found in Jos. 14:4; 1 Chron. 5:16; 13:2; 2 Chron. 11:16. The much rarer singular occurs in Lev. 25:34; Num. 35:2; Ez. 36:5; 45:2; 48:15, 17; 2 Chron. 31:19 (where both language and thought are related to Lev. 25:34).

(9) It is only in Num. 35:3 that the grazing lands are said to be *lbhmtm*, although the same point is made in other terms in Jos. 14:4. Levitical livestock is referred to expressly as *bhmt hlwym* only in Num. 3:45.

(10) *'l-py yhwh* occurs only in Jos. 17:4 and 15:13 (MT—LXX: *h'lhym*).

(11) We find talk of the lot 'going out' in Jos. 16:1 (MT); 18:11 (LXX); 19:1, 10 (LXX), 17, 24, 32, 40; 1 Chron. 24:7; 25:9.

(12) The only exact parallel to *'ḥzt bny yśr'l* is in Num. 35:8; while there are somewhat analogous uses of the prefaced *btwk* in Num. 32:30; 35:15; Jos. 14:3; 15:13; 16:9; 17:4, 6, 9; 19:9, 49; 20:9; 22:19.

Points 2, 7, and 8 may be taken to confirm our argument that the editor of Jos. 21 has worked from source material in Chronicles. And points 1 to 4 show that several links between our material and the Pentateuch are restricted to Num. 30–36.[18] It appears that Num. 30–31 and 36 may also have been influenced by this phase of the book of Joshua—perhaps through Num. 32–35. Then points 5, 10, 11, and 12 suggest that our editor has used language already in Joshua to blend with his material from Chronicles.

As for the shorter and apparently related passages in Joshua, 14:6a and 15:13 mention Joshua alone as the responsible agent; while the noun *ḥlḳ* of 15:13 is also used in Jos. 14:4; 18:5, 6, 7, 9; 19:9; 22:25, 27. It is not unlikely that the introductions to both Caleb-passages are presupposed by our editor of Jos. 21—cf. points 1 and 10 above. There are even more distinctive links in Jos. 17:4—cf. points 3, 6, 10, and 12.[19] In fact it is only their difference over one detail that makes us hesitate over positing the same stratum: in 17:4 it is over the *nśy'ym* that Eleazar and Joshua preside—contrast point 2 above. We have already noted in our previous chapter that these 'leaders' feature with them only in Num. 34:17—and with Eleazar's son Phinehas in Jos. 22:14. *nśy'ym* also appear in Joshua in 9:19, 21; 22:32; and, as *nśy'y h'dh*, in 9:15, 18 and 22:30. However, the term is quite common in the book of Numbers. Apart from the already noted problems of Num. 34,[20] it is used throughout the lists in chapters 2 and 7. The construction *nśy'y h'dh* is found in Num. 4:34; 16:2; 31:13; 32:2. Of the few further uses of the noun in Numbers[21] two seem of particular relevance to Jos. 17:4—Num. 27:2; 36:1. It is almost entirely from Num. 27:1–2 (with elements from vv. 4, 7) that Jos. 17:3–4 were apparently drafted—there Zelophehad's daughters petition Moses, Eleazar, the leaders, and the whole congregation.[22] Then in the opening of Num. 36, which returns to the legal decision of Num. 27, we find the men of the tribe addressing Moses (and Eleazar, in LXX and Syr) and *hnśy'ym r'šy 'bwt lbny yśr'l*—in this closing chapter of the book that immediately follows those chapters so heavily indebted to even late material in the book of Joshua, the term 'leaders' familiar throughout Numbers is apparently glossed with a phrase for clan chiefs found outside Chronicles only in late Joshua and the end of Numbers.

In fact it is only in Jos. 14:1b–3 that we find complete identity of language with the outer structure of Jos. 21—granted of course the difference in subject-matter. They share the expressions noted at 2, 3, 4, 6, and 12 above. Their likeness is the more marked, given the differences from both in 14:4–5.[23] These latter verses are clearly designed to make the earlier terminology perfectly clear. Whereas v. 3b has adopted *l' ntn nḥlh* from 13:14a, v. 4b—drawing on Jos. 21, while modifying its terminology—states more specifically *wl'-ntnw ḥlḳ llwym ky 'm-'rym lšbt. . . .*

The most economical hypothesis is that these five brief elements of later Joshua were drafted and added in the order in which they have been mentioned above. 14:6a and 15:13 portray Joshua alone as leader. It is the subject-matter of the opening of Jos. 17 that has prompted the import from 'Priestly' tradition in Num. 27 suggesting that Joshua like Moses had acted along with other senior colleagues. This phraseology is slightly modified by the editor of Jos. 21 who is naturally influenced by the milieu of his source. And it was this editor, or another very close to him, that drafted 14:1b–3, while 14:4–5 was added later.[24]

Only Jos. 19:51 remains to be considered. That verse—or at least v. 51a[25]—appears to depend on material already discussed rather than to belong to any stratum already discerned. It details the same officials as do 14:1b and 21:1, but refers to the tribal heads in a slightly different way—this is true however we construe *lmṭwt bny-yśr'l* that follows *r'šy h'bwt*: as a genitive linked to it, or as an indirect object after *nḥlw*.[26] Its use of the plural of *nḥlh* is unique in Joshua,[27]—as is its use of noun following demonstrative before the relative clause in such a summarizing verse.[28] If it resumes Jos. 14:1, then it resumes 18:1 too, with its mention of both Shiloh and the tent of meeting; while its addition of 'before Yahweh' shows that we are not dealing with simple correspondence. All in all, this appears an 'omnibus' conclusion to Jos. 14–19 drafted by a very late editor of the book.

So far then the nearest we have come to evidence of influence from 'Priestly' material in the Pentateuch on even the latest strata within Joshua has been our admission that the genealogical material in Jos. 17:1–2 about Machir/Manasseh seems to have prompted a cross-reference to Num. 27:1–2 (cf. 26:33). The editor of Jos. 21 (and 14:1b–3?) used some of this Pentateuchal material and the language of some other still conspicuous insertions into Joshua along with terminology from his major source as he adjusted and re-presented the Chronicler's information on Aaronite and Levitical holdings. Even Noth's admission[29] that we find in Joshua—not unexpectedly—isolated additions in the style and sense of P seems too strong. One of his indicators of P that we have not discussed here, the 'tent of meeting' in Jos. 18:1; 19:51, we have already shown to be used quite differently outside the Pentateuch from inside it.[30] Whether this represents adaptation from the Pentateuch, or separate development is unclear.

Lest any suspicion remain that unwelcome problems have been 'swept under the carpet' to serve this assertion that even Noth went too far[31] in conceding P-influence on Joshua, we must review briefly the use of three further terms in Jos. 21 and similar texts:

(1) I have argued elsewhere[32] that the phrase *lmšpḥt hḳhty* in 1 Chron. 6:39b—a phrase unique in the Chronicler's version of the tradition on the 'Levitic cities'—is one of several pointers that the following passage on Caleb and Hebron represents one of the very rare adjustments made to the Chronicler's version on the basis of Jos. 21. Not only are the Kohathite Levites referred to elsewhere in 1 Chron. 6 as *bny ḳht*, but *lmšpḥt hḳhty* of the parallel in Jos. 21:10 has already appeared in 21:4a—part of the Joshua editor's own introduction. Outside the three already mentioned verses, the patronymic is found only in Num. 3:27, 30; 4:18, 34, 37; 26:57;[33] 1 Chron. 6:18; 9:32; 2 Chron. 29:12. Only in Numbers is it construed with *mšpḥt*. In Num. 3 and 4 and 1 Chron. 6 the form alternates with *bny ḳht*. And while this evidence may just suffice to bolster my argument (already supported on other grounds) about Caleb and Hebron in 1 Chron. 6, it is certainly no

indicator of P-influence on Jos. 21.

(2) The fact that two of the passages under immediate scrutiny share a phrase with certain 'purple' P-passages in Genesis, such as chapters 17 and 23, makes appropriate a scrutiny of all its occurrences in the Bible. The 'land of Canaan' appears most often in Genesis—35 times[34]—as opposed to only 27 times elsewhere: Ex. 6:4; 16:35; Lev. 14:34; 18:3; 25:38; Num. 13:2, 17; 26:19; 32:30, 32; 33:40, 51; 34:2, 29; 35:10, 14; Deut. 32:49; Jos. 5:12; 14:1; 21:2; 22:9, 10, 11, 32; 24:3; Jud. 21:12; Ps. 105, 11 = 1 Chron. 16:18. Rendtorff has already observed that around half of the Genesis references (and so over a quarter of the total) occur in the Joseph story[35]—this is variously deemed early or late within the development of the Pentateuch, but never 'Priestly'.[36] In this story which is played out in two settings, the 'land of Canaan' appears both a natural label for Palestine and a natural contrast to Egypt. Many of its other occurrences are also in contrasts: (a) with Ur of the Chaldees and Paddan-Aram;[37] (b) with Lot's cities;[38] (c) with Esau's territory;[39] (d) with Transjordan—in Num. 32:30, 32 (33:51; 34:2, 29; 35:10); 35:14; Deut. 32:49; Jos. 14:1; 22:9, 10,11, 32; Jud. 21:12. It is the land of patriarchal promise and expectation—Gen. 17:8; 37:1; these may be 'Priestly' texts,[40] but the usage is foreshadowed in Jos. 24:3, a Deuteronomistic text. Then Jos. 5:12, another element of the Deuteronomistic History, concludes the story of the first passover after crossing the Jordan by noting that in that year Israel ate of the produce of the land of Canaan.[41] In the case of 'the land of Canaan' too, it may be that Jos. 21 shares terminology with P-strata of the Pentateuch; but it would go well beyond the evidence to claim influence from them.

(3) Discussion of our third term, *'ḥzh*, may tend to reopen that of *'rṣ kn'n* just concluded. It appears twice in Jos. 21: in one of the concluding notes (v. 41) referring to the holding[42] of the people of Israel, and in v. 12 on Caleb where *b'ḥztw* is a single word addition to the text of 1 Chron. 6:41.[43] Its only other occurrences in the book of Joshua are in chapter 22 (vv. 4, 9, 19 *bis*)—and the usage of the rare niph'al of the cognate verb in 22:9, 19[44] shows that the use of this term in Jos. 22 is quite self-conscious. The Pentateuchal usage is scattered and varied, though not frequent. It appears in Deut. 32:49.[45] Its use in Num. 35:2, 8, 28 is probably influenced by that in Jos. 21, and in Num. 32:22, 29, 32 (though probably not v. 5) by that in Jos. 22.[46] In that book that leaves only 27:4, 7.[47] In Leviticus we find it most often in two contexts—13 times in Lev. 25 and 5 times in Lev. 27—and apart from these only twice in Lev. 14:34. Then of its nine appearances in Genesis, five are related to the patriarchal tomb tradition—in the fixed phrase *'ḥzt-ḳbr*: 23:4, 9, 20; 49:30; 50:13; two promise Canaan to the patriarchs as an *'ḥzt 'wlm*—17:8; 48:4;[48] while 36:43 concludes the chapter on Esau/Edom and 47:11 describes Joseph settling his family in Egypt. Then apart from the isolated Ps. 2:8 and five references in the Chronicler, the fifteen occurrences in Ez. 44–48 are the only others in the Bible. From the clusters of references at the end of Leviticus and Ezekiel one may satisfy oneself about Gerleman's case[49] that *'ḥzh* means either 'holding' not in the sense of possession but of right to the usufruct, or 'cultivated land' as opposed to grazing. And this may be illustrated also in Gen. 47:11, possibly in Num. 35:28, and in our Jos. 21:12. It may be that Gen. 36 illustrates the intended sense of the self-conscious use of our term with cognate verb in Jos. 22 and Num. 32. Gen. 36:6 talks of Esau going to a land *opposite* Jacob, who is to remain in the 'land of Canaan'. It is the following synopsis of Edomite affairs that is concluded in 36:43 by *'lh 'lwpy 'dwm lmšbtm b'rṣ 'ḥztm*—what was not in the land of Canaan but was

still theirs by right. The Transjordanian tribes too face the tension of having rights across the river, granted by no less an authority than Moses, yet not living in *the* land. It is this situation that may help to explain the choice of terminology. Talk of Israel's enjoyment of Canaan as *'ḥzh*, which is naturally foreshadowed in Num. 32:30 and Jos. 22:19, appears in very few texts and can hardly be claimed as evidence of a 'Priestly' hand in Jos. 21:41.[50]

It remains our conclusion that the expansion of the opening of Jos. 17 was the only route by which certainly Pentateuchal 'Priestly' material entered Joshua—at least until the later influence of Num. 35:9–15 and perhaps other texts on Jos. 20.[51] However the twin 'P' imports of 'instruction through Moses' agency' and 'Joshua, Eleazar, and their associates' readily consolidated their position; and their presence in 14:1–5 and 19:51a has led many to claim these verses as the introduction and conclusion to the P-account in Joshua of the distribution of Canaan. But falsely.

D. Deuteronomy and Pentateuch

If the case for a contribution to the Joshua story from the continuation of the earlier strata now in the Pentateuch is, at the most, no further forward than Noth's dismissal left it in 1938; and if there was no *deliberate* influence on the book of Joshua from these 'Priestly' scholars who left their clear imprint on Genesis to Numbers; then evidence for Joshua ever having been associated with the developing Pentateuch—evidence for a (proto-) Hexateuch—is reduced almost to vanishing point. Certainly the development of Joshua had considerable influence on that of the closing chapters of Numbers. Yet that need in no way lead us to assume that both 'books' were part of the same unit during the relevant period. Indeed the use of 1 Chron. 6 in Jos. 21 (within quite a different stream of tradition) may be a good analogy for a contrary position.

Discussion has been renewed in recent years over the extent of Deuteronomistic influence within Genesis to Numbers.[52] It has never been found possible to deny all links between these books and the concerns of Deuteronomy.[53] And granted on the one side the complexity of the stratification of these books, and on the other the presence of Deuteronomistic-like elements in prophetic collections even outside the book of Jeremiah,[54] such influence on the emerging 'Tetrateuch' is hardly improbable. However Noth's insistence that in Deut. 1–3; 31; 34; Jos. 1ff. we see a new narrative begun retains its force. Smend's view is puzzling that the pre-'Priestly' 'Pentateuch' was linked with Deuteronomy—or, even more likely, with the Deuteronomistic History from Deuteronomy to Kings.[55] Finer distinction must be drawn between Deuteronomistic influence and Deuteronomistic composition/edition.

What may be said, then, about the production of our familiar Pentateuch? We noted in chapter V that Deuteronomy too, like Joshua, had influenced the production of at least Num. 33:50–35:15. That too need be no indication that both ‘books’ were part of the same literary unit. Indeed nothing seems to stand in the way of Sturdy’s suggestion[56] that the supplements at the end of Numbers were added before the separate book of Mosaic law in Deuteronomy was attached.[57] That link was very economically made, by suppressing the Numbers account of Moses’ death (influence from which has long been detected in Deut. 34), and by the familiar recapitulatory device after an insert of repeating and recasting Yahweh’s sentence from Num. 27:12–14 in Deut. 32:48–51.

The texts in parallel are as follows:

	Num. 27:12–14		*Deut. 32:48–51*
12	*wy’mr yhwh ’l-mšh*	*48*	*wydbr yhwh ’l-mšh*
			b‘ṣm hywm hzh l’mr
	‘lh ’l-hr h‘brym hzh	*49*	*‘lh ’l-hr h‘brym hzh*
			hr-nbw ’šr b’rṣ mw’b
			’šr ‘l-pny yrḥw
	wr’h ’t-h’rṣ		*wr’h ’t-’rṣ kn‘n*
	’šr ’ny ntty lbny yśr’l		*’šr ’ny nwtn lbny yśr’l l’ḥzh*
13	*wr’yth ’th*		
		50	*wmt bhr ’šr ’th ‘lh šmh*
	wn’spt ’l-‘myk gm ’th		*wh’sp ’l-‘myk*
	k’šr		*k’šr mt ’hrn ’ḥyk bhr hhr*
	n’sp ’hrn ’ḥyk		*wy’sp ’l-‘myw*
14	*k’šr mrytm py*	*51*	*‘l ’šr m‘ltm by btwk bny yśr’l*
			bmy-mrybt ḳdš
	bmdbr ṣn		*mdbr-ṣn*
	bmrybt h‘dh lhḳdyšny		*‘l ’šr l’ ḳdštm ’wty*
	bmym		
	l‘ynyhm		*btwk bny yśr’l*
	hm my mrybt ḳdš mdbr-ṣn		

It is noteworthy that LXX, and to a lesser extent Sam., offer a fuller version of Num. 27:12–14, so minimizing its differences from Deut. 32 (which is better attested textually).

The one text is clearly the point of departure for the other, which basically just annotates it throughout. To the introductory ‘And Yahweh said to Moses’[58] Deut. 32:48 adds ‘on that very day saying’.[59] And to ‘this mount Abarim’ it adds ‘mount Nebo, in the land of Moab, opposite Jericho’; while ‘see the land which I have granted to the people of Israel’ becomes ‘see the land *of Canaan* which I *am* granting to the people of Israel *as a holding* (*l’ḥzh*)’.[60] The relatively uncommon expression of Num. 27:13, ‘be gathered to one’s people’[61] is apparently explained in Deut. 32:50 by the common verb ‘die’—‘*and die on the mountain which you climb*, and be gathered to your people, as Aaron your brother *died on mount Hor, and* was gathered *to his people*’.[62] The differences between Num. 27:14 and Deut. 32:51 are rather greater: for *k’šr mrytm* (*’t-*)*py*[63] we have in the fuller version *‘l ’šr m‘ltm by btwk bny yśr’l*,[64] while the following *bmdbr ṣn* has prefaced to it *bmy-mrybt ḳdš*.[65] The first element of this added name appears in Num. 27:14’s specification of the rebellion: *bmrybt h‘dh lhḳdyšny bmym l‘ynyhm* (*hm my mrybt ḳdš mdbr-ṣn*). Deut. 32:51b offers instead a clause more closely parallel to v. 51a: *‘l ’šr l’ ḳdštm ’wty btwk bny yśr’l*. It is likely that this verse, though itself modelled on Num. 27:14, has in turn influenced its original. The double mention of the wilderness of Sin obtrudes in so tersely drafted a text as Num. 27:12–14. Then in the prior account of Aaron's death, *lhḳdyšny* is followed immediately by *lʿyny bny yśrʾl* (Num. 20:12), while the place-name is explained in the following verse—*hmh my mrybh ʾšr rbw. . . .* All in all, it seems not improbable that in *bmym* of Num. 27:14 we meet a misunderstanding of an abbreviation of *bmy m(rybh)* of 20:13. The apposition that now explains the unspecified 'waters' of the misunderstood and corrupted 27:14 has been drawn from the remodelled parallel in Deut. 32:51a where the episode has been localized at Kadesh, which is also implicitly connected with the wilderness of Sin. We have therefore good reason to believe that at both points where the Num. 27 text is longer than that in Deut. 32, the parent text has been brought into line with its offspring.

If the first draft of Num. 27:12–14 can be reconstructed with relative certainty, then the method and affinities of the recapitulation in Deut. 32:48–52 can be the more assuredly plotted. The various expansions and alterations cannot be reduced to a common denominator. And the clearest conclusion to emerge must be the negative one—that we do *not* see in Deut. 32:48ff. a blend of traditions from Numbers and Deuteronomy. *nʾsp ʾl ʿmyw* may require explanation, and *mrytm (ʾt-)py* alteration; but *mwt* is the commonest of verbs, while *mʿl* occurs only in Jos. 7:1 and 22:16, 31 within the 'Deuteronomistic' corpus; and is more 'at home' in Leviticus, Numbers, Ezekiel, and Chronicles. Then mount Hor appears only in Numbers; 'on that very day' occurs more often in the first three books of the Bible than elsewhere—and only in Jos. 5:11 can it be Deuteronomistic; while Kadesh is at home in both Numbers and Deuteronomy. If this recapitulatory notice is our clearest—and perhaps only—evidence of the work involved in giving our *Penta*teuch its present shape, then what happened at the time was no equal marriage of traditions but the introduction of Deuteronomy to the 'Priestly' harem—whatever we judge to have been the outcome of the union.

NOTES

1. Pp. 80–81.
2. *Die Kaleb-Traditionen im Alten Testament*, 1974.
3. Cf. chapter III above, p. 47.
4. *Kaleb-Traditionen*, p. 83.
5. In *RB* 78, pp. 5–17, 161–183, 321–354.
6. Langlamet had reviewed Mowinckel's *Quellenfrage* and *T-P-H* in *RB* 72 (1965).
7. In *RB* 79, pp. 7–38.
8. *Das Mazzotfest in Gilgal* (1975), pp. 26–198.
9. For further details, see my review of Otto in *VT* 28 (1978).
10. *Joshua, the Hebrew and Greek Texts*, pp. 22–28.
11. Cf. chapter III above, p. 43.
12. He agrees with Smend that vv. 7–9 are an addition, and argues too (*op. cit.*, p. 87) that v. 17b serves to bind the additional vv. 12–18 to the original introduction to Joshua in 1:1, 2, 5, 10, 11.

13. For his analysis of Num. 32 he is indebted to V. Fritz's *Israel in der Wüste* (1970), pp. 131f.
14. Tengström sub-titles *Die Hexateucherzählung* (1976) 'eine literaturgeschichtliche Studie' as a symbol of his claim that the business of literary criticism must be to interpret literary layers in the light of the presuppositions of the period and milieu of each.
15. For further details see below pp. 113–4, and also my review of Tengström in *JSOT* 8 (1978).
16. 'Der Untergang Jerichos (Jos. 6)', *Theologische Versuche* 8 (1977), pp. 11–20.
17. This I prefer to Japhet's opposite proposal that *mwšbwtm* reflects *'rym lšbt* of its 'source' in Jos. 21:3 (*JBL* 98, 1979). *mwšb*, whether in singular or plural, is much commoner and less remarkable than this rare phrase in Num. and Jos. While Japhet is correct (p. 215, n. 50) that its use in 1 Chron. (4:33; 6:39; 7:28) is only in passages linked with Jos., it is equally true that Jos. 17:11–13; 19:1–8; 21:1ff. are distinctive in their own setting. See further p. 118, n. 4.
18. 'Priestly' influence on these final chapters of Numbers is not to be denied; but it is manifested in elements other than those just listed.
19. Rather than *ḥlḳ* of 15:13, 17:4 uses the commoner *nḥlh*.
20. Cf. above, pp. 119–120, 126.
21. Cf. Num. 1:16; 3:24, 30, 32, 35; 13:2; 17:17, 21; 25:14, 18; 27:2; 36:1.
22. 'The whole congregation' is absent from 17:4; it is also the case that *'ḥzh* and *'ḥzt nḥlh* of Num. 27:4, 7 are represented in Jos. 17:4 by *nḥlh* alone.
23. *'t* for *byd* before *mšh*; *ḥlḳ* for *nḥl*; and *mḳnh* and *ḳnyn* for *bhmh*.
24. It is interesting that in their use of *ḥlḳ* these verses return to the usage of the original structure of the second half of Joshua—in 13:7 and the first draft of 19:49a.
25. The history of v. 51b has already been discussed above, pp. 65–66.
26. Genitival parallels were quoted on p. 94 above (at point 2). Another way of reading the verse (with the verb understood as a qal) was suggested above, p. 79. The phrase *r'šy h'bwt* is found independently in Ezra 2:68; 3:12; 4:2; Neh. 7:69, 70; 12:12, 23; 1 Chron. 7:1; 23:24; 26:32; 27:1; 2 Chron. 1:2.
27. The only other Biblical example being in Is. 49:8.
28. The few parallels to this uncommon construction are in Num. 36:13; Ez. 41:22; 48:29; Ezra 1:3—two of which are verses that conclude books.
29. *Josua*², p. 11.
30. In chapter IV above, p. 63.
31. Much Biblical criticism since Noth has viewed him as such a destructive minimalist that 'even Noth agrees/concedes' has often been used as a guarantee of accuracy.
32. In 'Cities of Refuge in Israelite Tradition', *JSOT* 10 (1978).
33. Num. 26:57 may in fact be later than Jos. 21. It opens a new section, after the conclusion of the main list by the notice on land-division.
34. Gen. 11:31; 12:5 (*bis*); 13:12; 16:3; 17:8; 23:2, 19; 31:18; 33:18; 35:6; 36:5, 6; 37:1; 42:5, 7, 13, 29, 32; 44:8; 45:17, 25; 46:6, 12, 31; 47:1, 4, 13, 14, 15; 48:3, 7; 49:30; 50:5, 13.
35. *Problem des Pentateuch* (1977), p. 119.
36. The less common case for a later dating has been most cogently advanced in Redford's *A Study of the Biblical Story of Joseph*, SVT 20 (1970).
37. Gen. 11:31; 12:5; 31:18; 33:18; 48:7.
38. Gen. 13:12.
39. Gen. 36:5, 6.
40. Rendtorff has contested (cf. p. 142, n. 35 above), as others before him, the adequacy of evidence for an isolable P-document in Genesis.
41. I have argued, in 'Joshua: the Hebrew and Greek Texts', that, once (on the

evidence of the LXX) the Hebrew text has been freed of later additions, the evidence of 'Priestly' influence on the original vanishes. This verse could provide another example of a contrasting use of 'the land of Canaan'.

42. Cf. below on the meaning of the term.
43. It was suggested on page 96 and n. 32, that the note on Caleb was the sole import from Jos. 21 into 1 Chron. 6. If so, then either *b'ḥztw* was omitted (which is unlikely as there are other differences between the two notes) or it represents a late addition to Jos. 21.
44. Found, apart from the related Num. 32:30, only in Gen. 22:13; 34:10; 47:27; and Eccles. 9:12.
45. Cf. section *D* below—that verse also mentions 'the land of Canaan'.
46. One thinks not just of the similarity of the situations, but also the use of the cognate verb *n'ḥz*—cf. n. 44 above.
47. Already mentioned in our discussion of Jos. 17:3–4 on p. 95 above.
48. Cf. Lev. 25:34—and almost certainly associated in Gen. 17 with the much commoner expression *bryt 'wlm*.
49. 'Nutzrecht und Wohnrecht', *ZAW* 89 (1977).
50. Cf. Gen. 17:8; 48:4; Lev. 14:34; Deut. 32:49—all already mentioned.
51. Discussed in chapter V, p. 80.
52. Some of the more significant discussions are C. Brekelmans, 'Die sogenannte deuteronomistische Elemente in Genesis bis Numeri', *Geneva Congress Volume*, SVT 15 (1966); W. Fuss, *Die deuteronomistische Pentateuchredaktion in Ex. 3–17*, BZAW 126 (1972); P. Weimar, *Untersuchungen zur Redaktionsgeschichte des Pentateuch*, BZAW 146 (1977).
53. 'Even Noth' (cf. p. 101, n. 31 above) did not do so.
54. Deuteronomistic influence on the production of the book of Jeremiah is widely accepted. For other collections, one has in mind for example Wolff's reading of Amos which has sparked general sympathetic comments in Clements' *Prophecy and Tradition* (1975), pp. 41–57.
55. *Die Entstehung des Alten Testaments* (1978), p. 63.
56. *Numbers*, p. 196—cf. p. 45 above.
57. The separateness of Deuteronomy as a corpus over against developing 'Tetrateuchal' tradition seems emphasized rather than the reverse by the apparent acquaintance of parts of Deut. 1–3 with some of the desert traditions in Numbers. These may have served as sources, but they have also been left unedited—at least by the Deuteronomists.
58. The verbs of speaking differ in MT but not in Sam.
59. Sam also represents *l'mr* in Num. 27:12. *b'ṣm hywm hzh* is found in Gen. 7:13; 17:23, 26; Ex. 12:17, 41, 51; Lev. 23:21, 28, 29, 30; Jos. 5:11; Ez. 24:2; 40:1.
60. Mount Nebo is detailed also in Deut. 34:1, where it is further described as *r'š hpsgh*. The second supplement in 32:49 is paralleled only in Lev. 14:34 (with 'to you' for 'to the people of Israel').
61. Found only in Gen. 25:8, 17; 35:29; 49:29, 33; Num. 20:24, 26; 31:2.
62. A further difference that English translation camouflages is that Deut. 32:49, 50 offer a series of four co-ordinate imperatives, while Num. 27:12 has offered the first two of these ('go up' and 'see') but in v. 13 has repeated the latter in the form of a *waw*-consecutive with perfect, which construction is continued for 'and be gathered'. We might reconstruct an earlier draft of Num. 27 as having opened with but one imperative form, followed by *wr'yth 't-h'rṣ . . .*—this had been partially displaced by the imperative preferred by the later editor in Deut. 32:49.
63. The phrase *mrh ('t-)py* is found only in Num. 20:24; 27:14; 1 Sam. 12:15; 1 Kings 13:21, 26; Lam. 1:18.
64. Within the Pentateuch, *m'l b-* is used also in Lev. 5:15, 21; 26:40; and Num.

5:6, 12, 27. It is found in Joshua in 7:1 and 22:16, 31. And, apart from Dan. 9:7 and Prov. 16:10, the other occurrences are 7 in Ezekiel, and 15 in the Chronicler.

65. The wilderness of Sin—known also from Num. 13:21; 20:1; 33:36; 34:3; and Jos. 15:1—is nowhere else linked with the waters of Meribah (of Kadesh).

CHAPTER VII

RETROSPECT AND PROSPECT

A. The Argument Reviewed

I. Von Rad's 1938 essay on the Hexateuch sought to explain the overall shape of a given literary complex: the books Genesis to Joshua. Up to that date critical scholarship was certain about the delimitation of that complex, certain that Joshua was the conclusion of the Pentateuch. The publication in the same year of Noth's commentary on Joshua might well have resulted in the shattering of that literary consensus, had it not been for von Rad. Such was the power of his form-critical and traditio-historical argumentation that Noth in later studies was apparently not prepared to press the logic of his own literary conclusions about the relations between the book of Joshua and the final chapters of Numbers. He did not question *whether* the earlier strata of Pentateuchal tradition had had as their goal an account of Israel's settlement in Canaan, but only whether that account had been *preserved*. In their further work on Pentateuch/Hexateuch, and in their critique of each other's work, the minds of both von Rad and Noth were exercised over how to distinguish in practice literary criticism on the one side and form-criticism and traditio-history on the other.

II. This was quite as explicit a concern of Mowinckel. His support for von Rad's essay on the Hexateuch was matched by his admiration for Noth's demonstration of the importance of the contribution made by the Deuteronomist to the traditions of Joshua and the succeeding Former Prophets. Mowinckel's own attempt to restate the Hexateuch hypothesis is the harder to evaluate, marred as it is by many blemishes in the detail of his argument. He was also influenced, even more than von Rad, by a belief about basic constancy of form and fixity of tradition. This *a priori* conviction is hard to prove or disprove; but its attractiveness is lessened by its apparent practical concomitant in the work of both scholars: less than fair description of some of the key texts under scrutiny.

III. Nowhere has the influence of Noth, and of his teacher Alt, been more apparent than in the study of the topographical data within the second half of Joshua. And nowhere have detailed successor studies evidenced more striking contrariety in their results. Many of these studies testify to the extraordinary literary complexity of Jos. 13–21. This often despite themselves; for 'biblical geographers' have often shown little literary appreciation of the consequences of their sifting, and occasionally manipulating, parts of the evidence. It is from Noth's work that most subsequent detailed study of Joshua has taken its inspiration, even where many of his own detailed arguments have been rebutted or where his own literary sensitivity has been lacking. In this respect, some of the standard Introductions to the Old Testament are quite out of step with the more specialized literature, which now shows little predisposition to analyze the book of Joshua in terms of the hypotheses of Pentateuchal criticism. Scholars still so disposed should consider closely three points from the first half of this present study: (1) its conclusion that Noth's analysis of Num. 32 is insufficiently radical; (2) its complaint that Mowinckel's arguments about both Num. 32 and Jud. 1 are very muddled; and (3) its challenge to von Rad's and Mowinckel's assumptions about tenacity of form and the basic fixity of 'Hexateuchal' tradition.

IV. Our own fresh study of the second half of the book of Joshua suggested that the main narrative stratum of that book did in fact offer an account of the distribution by Joshua of the land west of the Jordan to ten tribes, with a preliminary note about Moses' Transjordanian grant to two more. This account was first adjusted and supplemented gradually. Then later a thorough reorganization of the material was made: (a) Manasseh and Ephraim became treated as but subsections of Joseph; (b) Judah and Joseph were held to have settled before the other western tribes; (c) it was made clear that it had been *by lot* that the remaining seven tribes had received their holdings. Further brief supplements and adjustments were made, one of them assigning northern Transjordan to part of Manasseh, while another made clear that the principle of lot applied to all the western tribes. The two larger appendices, on cities for the Levites and of refuge for the manslayer, are close to the end of the development of the tradition common to MT and LXX in Joshua.

V. As for the last ten or so chapters of Numbers, these we found to be more dependent on the second half of Joshua than even Noth had supposed. Their earliest mention of the division of the land is apparently a statement of Mosaic authority for the division of the land as described in the first main narrative stratum of Joshua. Succeeding passages equally attribute to Moses a series of warnings and instructions modelled on successive stages of the expanding Joshua report. The latest elements in Num. 26–36 dealing with the land owe as much as the earliest to corresponding developments in the parent (i.e. Joshua) text. These findings are of considerable significance: (a) they help to confirm our analysis of Joshua; and (b) they throw light on both the source and the function of much of the material on 'the land' at the end of the book of Numbers.

VI. Finally, we took account of a number of recent studies that detected continuations in Joshua of earlier narrative strata within the Pentateuch, finding all of them unconvincing; and reviewed those latest elements in

Joshua often claimed to evidence the presence or at least influence of Pentateuchal 'P', seeking to explain these in other terms. Taken along with our discussions in chapters I–III of earlier studies in this last generation, this amounts to a rebuttal of the Hexateuch hypothesis, and encourages an explanation of the formation of the Pentateuch distinct from that of Joshua to Kings. As a first contribution to this, we discussed the incorporation of Deuteronomy into 'Priestly' tradition to complete the Pentateuch much as we know it.

B. Sources and Dating

Following this rather formal review of the argument so far, it seems appropriate now to recapitulate and develop some of its conclusions and observations about the development of the biblical tradition on the distribution of Israel's land. This will help clarify at least a relative dating of the relevant materials, and will consider the sources available at each stage of the tradition.

(1) We suggested, admittedly only on the analogy of what demonstrably happened later in the tradition, that the first draft of the second half of Joshua underlies the first note in Numbers about the distribution of the land: that Num. 26:52–54 describes briefly, as a programme revealed to Moses, the essentials of the earliest version of Jos. 13–19. The keyword is *ḥlḳ* (Num. 26:53; Jos. 13:7 and the original text of Jos. 19:49a)—'divide'—and it is made clear that the divisions vary in size, as do the tribes themselves. Jos. 13–19* is then the main source of Num. 26:52–54. All that is added is the doctrine (not explicit at this stage in the Joshua tradition, and so not demonstrably assumed there) that Moses fore-ordained the distribution of the land; the rest is mere deduction from the account in Joshua.

The details of that Joshua account we have not yet specified too precisely. On the basis of the use of a subsequent draft in Numbers and also at the beginning of Judges, it was argued that the original order of the tribal divisions was: Judah, Simeon, Benjamin, Dan, Manasseh, Ephraim, Zebulun, Issachar, Asher, Naphtali. It was also noted that the final six tribes listed (those of the centre and north) have their territories described in rather different language from the others. The use of *pgʿ b-*/'touch' in all six and nowhere else has already been mentioned. The negative point may also be relevant, that they do not make use of two of the ten verbs listed in Bächli's discussion of the development of Jos. 13–19—*pnh*/'turn' and *tʾr*/'make a detour'.[1] It may finally be noted that one of the two commonest verbs in the other topographical descriptions in these chapters scarcely appears in connection with the 'six'.[2] It may well be, therefore, that the information about the central and northern tribes in the first draft of Joshua came from a different source from that which supplied the details about Judah and her more immediate neighbours.[3]

(2) What we have described as the second stage in the development of the tradition in Joshua had two aspects:

(a) A series of additions were made to the first version of Jos. 13–19, emphasizing the incompleteness of the conquest achieved: the land remaining to be fully possessed (13:2–6a); the sharing of part of Trans-jordan (13:13); the enclaves on the west at Jerusalem (15:63), Gezer (16:10), Ayyalon and Shaalbim (19:47—LXX), and to the north of Manasseh (17:11–13).[4] These additions culminate in the whole of Jos. 23, which makes clear the religious consequences of a less than complete dis-possession of the original Canaanite population.

(b) Personal allocations to Joshua (19:49b–50) and Caleb (15:13–19) were described.

For most of these additions the editors presumably had detailed information available—but not necessarily the kind of archival source-material often thought to underly the so-called 'list of unconquered cities' in Jud. 1:21, 27–35. It is likely that the note on Joshua's own town is a deduction from the account of his death and burial in the first draft of the material—there (Jos. 24:30=Jud. 2:9) Timnath-heres is described as being north of Mount Gaash, as if relatively unknown, while in the later Jos. 19:50 no such specification is necessary. Then the Jebusite hold on Jerusalem till the time of David was well known, while Canaanite occupa-tion of Gezer in Solomon's reign is attested in 1 Kings.[5] As for the longer note on Caleb, a connection between Caleb and Hebron (Jos. 15:13) is made too in the spy-story in Num. 13:22, which also mentions the three sons of Anak (15:14). However the following anecdote about Achsah, Othniel, and the Negeb springs is without biblical connection, apart from its repetition in Jud. 1.

It was this stage of the Joshua tradition that served as a primary source for two other compositions: the first draft of Num. 33:50–34:29, and Jud. 1.

In this return to the theme of land-distribution in Numbers, the order in which the tribal representatives are listed could of course have been drawn from the first draft of Joshua; but some of the language earlier in this Numbers passage shows its author familiar with an expanded Joshua.

I have argued at length elsewhere that Jud. 1 is dependent on Joshua at all points where it offers similar or identical material; and it happens that much of the Joshua material so used is from the supplements added at this second stage. The Caleb story was 'Judahized' (and possibly also the story about Adonizedek of Jerusalem in Jos. 10); while documentation of foreign enclaves was turned to good effect in a largely negative account of unsuccessful settlement in the area of the northern kingdom.[6]

(3) Jud. 1 is of course not only inspired by material from Joshua. As is hardly surprising in a fresh introduction for the probably now separate *book* of Judges[7] it has been influenced by other material in that book too.

Judah's difficulties in the plain because of 'iron chariots' (1:19) remind us of Sisera's dreaded forces (4:3, 13). Treatment of Dan as the northernmost tribe (1:34–35) will be in deference to the extended account of that tribe's migration in Jud. 17–18. I have already noted[8] that the replacement by 'house of Joseph' (1:35) of 'Ephraim' in Jos. 19:47 (LXX) suggests that 'house of Joseph' functions as a rubric for all the material in Jud. 1:22–35. Finally, talk in the opening three verses of oracular consultation of God, Judah's priority, and the associated mention of *gwrl*/'lot' are all parallelled in 20:9, 18; like the handling of Dan, all these may be inspired by the traditions now at the close of the book.

All these observations permit this new suggestion: that Jud. 1, itself heavily dependent on the second stage of the drafting of Joshua, has contributed to the fundamental reshaping of the second half of Joshua at stage three. This redrafting of Joshua has a number of aspects; and elements in each of them appear to have been foreshadowed in the composition of Jud. 1:

(a) The second of the two additional passages that portray the once separate Manasseh and Ephraim as parts of greater Joseph, 17:14–18, is repetitive and says little.[9] If it is a fresh composition designed to explain the division of Joseph into two parts, then we may plausibly see influence from Jud. 1 at two points—the use of *gwrl* in vv. 14, 17 (cf. Jud. 1:3), and mention of Canaanite opposition with 'chariots of iron' in vv. 16, 18 (cf. Jud. 1:19).

(b) The prominence in Jud. 1 of Judah, vis-à-vis Simeon, and Joseph, vis-à-vis the other central and northern tribes, may have contributed to the way in which they are dealt with first in Jos. 15–17 and become points of reference for the other tribes in Jos. 18:5, 11b; 19:1b.

(c) The repeated mention in Jos. 18:1–10 that the decisive action will take place 'before Yahweh' and its statement that the allocation will be 'by lot' may both be influenced by Jud. 1:1–3 (if not directly by Jud. 20:9, 18).

(d) Dan's position at the end of Jos. 19 may well have been suggested by the similar transposition in Jud. 1.

This line of argument goes quite a long way to making conceivable just how, and in part why, the substantial reconstruction of the book of Joshua[10] at this third stage was effected. Our suggestion that Jos. 17:14–18 and 18:1–10 are new 'purpose-built' narratives may commend some caution before accepting all Bächli's interesting suggestions on the relations between official commissions and the form in which the tribal territories are described in Jos. 13–19.[11] If Jos. 18:1–10 considerably post-dates the surrounding information, it may be evidence of an earlier version of Bächli's own deduction—but equally it would be wrong to use it as evidence of the *validity* of this deduction, or as a tool to reconstruct lists *behind* the present form of the territorial descriptions.

(4) I can offer no elucidation of the source of the tradition about half-Manasseh in northern Transjordan. Yet, that this marked a late development in both Joshua and Numbers is one of the most secure results of our study of these books in chapters IV and V above.[12]

(5) I have argued in detail elsewhere that the source of Jos. 21:1–42 is to be found in 1 Chron. 6:39–66—with the exception of the note on Caleb and Hebron[13] which is an isolated example of influence in the opposite direction. All the Chronicler's text is re-used in Jos. 21. The Chronicler's account of cities for Aaronites and Levites was the product of gradual and rather haphazard development. What we find in Joshua is a re-organization and re-presentation of this material in a more ordered structure, and as the fulfilment of a divine command through Moses.[14]

It is important to stress that it is not by chance that it is among the tribal and genealogical traditions at the beginning of the Chronicler's history that we find the source of the material in Joshua on the Levitical cities. It was not by lucky accident that the Chronicler preserved a text which had already served its purpose as the source of Jos. 21, or indeed as an earlier draft of that chapter. Two kinds of consideration lead to the conclusion that 1 Chron. 6:39–66 is a product of its own milieu.

It makes a much clearer distinction than Jos. 21 between Aaronites and Levites, between Judah, or the southern area, and the rest of the country. These distinctions have been skilfully and economically played down by the Joshua editor, without actually departing from his source-text.[15] It is these distinctions that are so much at home in Chronicles: (a) 1 Chron. 9:2 distinguishes between priests and Levites in its four categories of Jerusalem settlers—Israel, priests, Levites, and temple servants. (b) 1 Chron. 13:2 operates with a similar distinction when it records the sending of a message 'to all our brethren who remain in all the land of Israel and with them to the priests and Levites in the cities that have pasture lands'. (c) In 2 Chron. 11:14 we learn of the Levites leaving their holdings and coming to Judah and Jerusalem. (d) Finally, 2 Chron. 31:11ff. tells of Hezekiah (in a Judahite context) arranging a distribution to Aaronites in the cities of the priests.

Our second consideration is this. 1 Chron. 6:39–66 is a rather arbitrarily defined text. It is only the similarity of these verses to Jos. 21:1–42 that has encouraged critics to view them as a unit. Looked at in their own context, they are only part of a much fuller tradition about Aaronites and Levites that has grown by supplementation rather than been planned. This, together with our earlier point that its distinctions are familiar elsewhere in Chronicles, makes it likely that it has undergone this development within its present context.

It is then a Chronicles text in the full sense that has served as the source for Jos. 21:1–42; and Jos. 21 we have shown to be the source of Num. 35:1–8*, which like preceding sections of the end of Numbers attributes to divine command through Moses the explanation of what is to occur once the land is taken.[16]

In 1 Chron. 6, and perhaps in the first draft of Jos. 21 too, all the cities listed are described as *ʿry hmḳlṭ*/'the cities of "refuge"'. Either the Chronicler meant something other than 'refuge' by *mḳlṭ*, or he had a different understanding of the legal provisions for refuge cities from that now clearly enunciated in the closely related Jos. 20 and Num. 35:9ff.[17] These chapters are entirely in the spirit of the Deuteronomic law on refuge (enunciated in 19:1ff. and 4:41–43), and use its terminology of 'cities to which the slayer may flee' interchangeably with 'cities of *mḳlṭ*' inherited from the Chronicler. How far this modifies the otherwise unknown term *mḳlṭ* and how far it emphasizes a more limited provision of refuge-cities is far from clear. What is clear is that Deuteronomy and Chronicles are the twin sources of the account given of refuge in Num. 35 and Jos. 20.

The first clear implication of this review is that virtually all the addition of information or alteration of perspective which we have shown that the first draft of Joshua's account of land division underwent had its immediate source in other (now) biblical material—and material much in the same form as we know it. Negatively this means that hypothetical 'sources' reconstructed by 'literary critics' are not required to explain this material. More positively it seems to imply that over a certain period those who preserved the book of Joshua[18] took account of relevant material shaped in other circles, and occasionally used it to reshape or expand what they recognized as the normative account of the allocation of Canaan to Israel. In other words, Joshua functioned as some sort of 'canonical' repository for all relevant information. A similar situation obtains at the end of the book of Numbers. There, the immediate source for the developing tradition to be found in 26:52–56; 33:50–34:29; and 35 is the book of Joshua. Those who preserved the Moses-traditions had a parallel concern: to assert the master's authority for every detail of the dispositions made by his successor in the land.

The second clear implication is that considerable caution is required by the historian who would handle this material. Much less of it has been transcribed from archives than many historians of early Israel have allowed. Much of the material under review is not raw source-data for the modern historian, but rather the solutions and deductions of his counterparts in the later biblical period—of quite as much interest, of course, once recognized for what they are!

A third series of implications concerns relative dating. The point of departure for all the material under review is the first draft of the Joshua narrative; and we have seen no evidence leading us to query Noth's ascription of this narrative to an author or circle influenced by Deuteronomy once that work had become normative—implying a date later in the Judaean monarchy or early in the exile. It is on a revision of this narrative that Jud. 1 depends. Finally, the ultimate dependence of Num. 35 on material that developed within 1 Chron. 6 and in the spirit of other traditions in the Chronicler's history seems to have this implication, assuming that the books of Chronicles and Ezra-Nehemiah are the product of the same author(s) or at least period: that either the Pentateuch was not 'canonized' as early as Ezra, or the Pentateuch although an official code under Ezra was still open to new material.[19]

C. Tetrateuch–Pentateuch–Hexateuch

Mention of the Pentateuch is a convenient signal that it is opportune to conclude our study with an explicit return to the problem implied in its sub-title. This is not the place for an extended discussion. But we shall mention how our results relate to three recent studies of the Pentateuch, and suggest some wider issues.[20]

(1) *Rendtorff*

Rendtorff's[21] new impulse to Pentateuchal criticism has already provoked a good deal of published comment;[22] and there is no place here for an extended review. What can be done is to note (a) that our discussion of the tradition of the division of the land is somewhat analogous to Rendtorff's remarks on the gradual development and adjustment of some Pentateuchal traditions; and (b) that our detailed conclusions about the end of Numbers and the completion of the Pentateuch call for a reappraisal of his conclusions on these points.

(a) Rendtorff is surprised too that Noth's understanding of the growth of the Pentateuch was not more radically affected by his conclusions about Joshua and the end of Numbers. He is right to describe as highly precarious[23] Noth's argument that the end of the story in the earlier Pentateuchal 'sources' was pruned in the interest of an overall edition based on a Priestly Document that had concluded with reports on the deaths of Miriam, Aaron, and Moses—and was subsequently lost. His own preference is to ascribe as much initial independence to the larger units of tradition within the Pentateuch (on the primeval history, patriarchs, exodus, and the like) as Noth did to the settlement traditions within Joshua. He has no place for a creative theologian, the 'Yahwist', of the early monarchy. It was only much later—and then not very systematically—that these units were brought together in circles close to or even part of the Deuteronomic movement. Even the 'Priestly' contribution to the Pentateuch is far from uniform. Rendtorff prefers to talk of Priestly texts than a Priestly narrative; and his remarks about their piecemeal elaboration in Genesis and Exodus are not at all dissimilar to our account of methods of composition in Joshua and the end of Numbers.

(b) It is only at the end of his book that Rendtorff explicitly broaches topics we have discussed above.[24] He draws attention to the clear presence of 'Deuteronomistic' elements in Num. 32–35; and finds it obvious that no strict separation can be made between the book of Deuteronomy and the rest of the 'Tetrateuch'—the announcement of Moses' death in Num. 27:12–23 and the report of its occurrence in Deut. 34 show that the connection of the two is intended. He concludes against Noth that it is far from certain that a 'Pentateuch' once had independent existence without Deuteronomy, and was linked with Deuteronomy and possibly the Deuteronomistic History only in a later editorial action. On the contrary Rendtorff insists that the very problems produced by the mutual relationships between the final chapters of Numbers, Deuteronomy, and the the 'Deuteronomistic' settlement-tradition show that the 'Deuteronomistic' element clearly played an important role in the combination of the different components of tradition in this sphere.

Several aspects of this account require challenge. Our own scrutiny of the end of Numbers would lead to more than caution in describing Joshua's contribution to Numbers as 'Deuteronomistic'—firstly, because the structure of these chapters is thoroughly 'Priestly'; and then, because much of the material contributed is from strata in Joshua later than can be usefully described as 'Deuteronomistic'.[25] Next, the lines of influence we detected (whether of material in Joshua on material in Numbers, or of 'Priestly'/ 'Pentateuchal' incorporation first of the material at the end of Numbers and then of Deuteronomy as a whole) are so uniform as to render suspect Rendtorff's talk of *mutual* relationships. It is, lastly, surprising that he seeks to relate Num. 27 and Deut. 34 on the death of Moses without a mention of the intervening and recapitulating Deut. 32:48–52. That passage makes clear that a connection between the other two is intended—but equally clear that this connection was a novelty in terms of the development of Deuteronomy. Our own remarks have noted just how *little* the 'book' of Deuteronomy appears to have been influenced by its attachment to the rest of the Pentateuch.

Just one final caution about Rendtorff's varied evidence of 'Deuteronom(ist)ic' influence on Genesis-Numbers, leading to the restatement of the theory of a Deuteronomic redaction extending over all the books from Genesis to Kings. Though properly cautious over the criteria for terming various terms and texts 'Deuteronomic', he welcomes the attention paid by Vriezen to the striking parallelism between the beginning of the Exodus story and the beginning of the stories of the Judges (Ex. 1:6, 8 and Jud. 2:8, 10). Given these examples of the same literary schema used to mark the transition between two distinct periods Rendtorff rejects as hardly likely that we are dealing with a literary form which had an existence independent of a particular circle of authors; his conclusion follows that those responsible for Ex. 1 and Jud. 2 belonged to the same Deuteronom(ist)ic circle. Yet, even granted his negative point, an alternative explanation is possible: that those who drafted Ex. 1 knew Jud. 2:8, 10 (as part of a text, not an independent literary form), just as those who drafted Num. 26:52–54 knew the terminology for land-division used in the first version of Jos. 13–19 (almost certainly the same Deuteronomistic stratum as Jud. 2:6–10!). Perhaps even more caution is required than even Rendtorff recognizes in the detection of Deuteronom(ist)ic influence on Genesis-Numbers.

(2) *Tengström*
In the introduction to his study of the narrative of the Hexateuch Tengström too protests against the unlikelihood of Noth's (and Engnell's) sharp differentiation between 'Tetrateuch' and 'Deuteronomistic History'.[26] He scorns the remarkable coincidence that precisely the section on the settlement, so inexplicably left out by both the original P-source and the editor who inserted the older sources into the P-source, should be available—though in another version—at the beginning of the completely independent Deuteronomistic work. Tengström admits that there are only traces of P in Joshua. but regards as a frivolous evasion of the difficulty Noth's disposal of these as isolated additions in the style of P: what is held to be in the style of P must belong to the P-stratum, because elsewhere it is precisely stylistic criteria that are used to decide just which literary stratum or source a text belongs to. As for 'Deuteronomistic' traces in Genesis-Numbers, he gives some support to Brekelmans' argument that some of these are rather 'pre-Deuteronomistic' and depend on an 'Elohistic' tradition from northern Israel which was the immediate source of the originally northern Deuteronomists.[27] A stress on the remarkable continuity between the older strata in the Pentateuch and earlier phases of the Deuteronomic tradition is important in any estimation of the book of Joshua. The conclusion Tengström draws is that the relationship of the books of Moses to the following historical books is significantly more complicated than Noth and Engnell assumed, and that this problem is unlikely to find any solution unless the 'Hexateuch' is somehow recognized as an original unit. Like Rendtorff, he is inclined to deny that an independent P-source ever existed: the P-stratum is not a source, but a series of expansions concentrated in the first four books and much more sporadic thereafter. But unlike him he ascribes the kernel of the 'Hexateuch'—and a substantial one at that—not to the end of the monarchy, nor to its early stages, but to circles associated with Shechem before the rise of David. And the main part of his book studies the structure of this supposed primary narrative.[28]

Tengström is surely mistaken to criticize Noth's distinction between isolated additions in the style of P and P itself, supposing that the latter did exist. Influence must be distinguished in principle from authorship. Then even granted the denial of an independently existing P-source, his distinction between concentrated Priestly expansions in Genesis-Numbers and more sporadic activity in Joshua is far short of an adequate contrast of the literary situation in these texts. And as for links at an earlier stage between Joshua and the narrative of the Pentateuch, these Tengström demonstrates at the cost of terming parts of Deut. 31:1–8; 34:1–8 and Jos. 1 pre-Deuteronomic and assigning them to his primal narrative of the Hexateuch. Apart from the fact that these few passages, with some verses from Num. 32 conveniently fill a large gap between the middle of Numbers and Jos. 2, his only argument for denying that these few verses *within Deuteronomy* and the opening of Joshua are 'Deuteronomic' is that they have been supplemented by obviously Deuteronomic material.[29]

(3) *Clines*

Clines offers a very sensitive defence of his proposal that the theme of the Pentateuch *as it stands* 'is the partial fulfilment—which implies also the partial non-fulfilment—of the promise to or blessing of the patriarchs. . . . The promise has three elements: posterity, divine-human relationship, and land.'[30] The first of these elements Clines finds to predominate in Genesis 12–50, the second in Exodus-Leviticus, and the third in Numbers-Deuteronomy. It is only in his penultimate chapter that Clines turns briefly to the literary history of the Pentateuch with a discussion of two aspects of its final theme—the concept of a promise, and the concept of an only partial fulfilment of the patriarchal promises. Here he notes the clear stance of Deuteronomy between promise and fulfilment, and records the majority opinion that the Priestly Work looks to the future, with its 'assurance that the cult will be revived, and that in the land of promise'. Assessment of the Yahwist's intentions are complicated by scholarly disagreement over his conclusion—reaffirmation of the promise of blessing in the Balaam episode, or fulfilment of the promise of land in a (lost?) settlement account.

We have already sought to defend the view that evidence is absent even from the end of Numbers that the Yahwist was concerned to report Israel's settlement in the promised land (or even a token settlement in Transjordan). The last substantial element of pre-Priestly tradition in Numbers is the Balaam cycle. What is most significant there is Balaam's resolute refusal to curse a people blessed by Yahweh. So extensively is this theme presented that the silence of the relevant three chapters of Numbers on the topic of land is quite deafening. The solitary mention (24:18) of a possession of Edom/Seir appears in a prediction of the far future (24:17—David?) not of imminent settlement. For actual talk of the land as a goal in the earlier strata of Numbers, we have to reach back to the request to Hobab for company on the way through the desert, to the backward looks to Egypt and revolts against Moses, and to the despatch of the spies into Canaan (Num. 10–14, *passim*). Clines may be right that if there was a Yahwist, and if his work ended at Balaam not the settlement, then we may ascribe to the Yahwist the thematic element of 'promise awaiting fulfilment'. It would be much harder to claim that land was the most prominent aspect of that promise in the earlier strata of Numbers.

In fact if our own analysis holds, it was only in the final stages of the production of the Pentateuch that 'the land' came to loom so large as Clines shows it does. If we detach Deuteronomy and the final nine chapters of Numbers, then much of Clines' documentation vanishes with them. And what remains in Num. 1–27 appears in a new light once shorn of its massive appendix. Apart from the already mentioned invitation to Hobab, the land is not once mentioned as the goal of the preparations described in the first ten chapters—for departure from Sinai, onward movement, camp life, and war. In the chapters that follow there is some specifically 'Priestly' mention of the land as the goal; but it is far from dominant. Its significance may best be grasped in chapters 20 and 27, on the deaths of Aaron and Moses, and the succession of Eleazar and Joshua. The punishment of Moses and Aaron for rebellion is that they will not lead the assembly of Israel into the land granted them by God (20:12), and in fact will die outside that land (20:24; 27:13) though Moses will come in sight of it (27:12). The land plays a part in these episodes, but it could hardly be said to dominate. And its lack of significance for the author is clearest in his immediately following account of the institution of Joshua as successor to Moses (27:15–23): his suitability and authority are noted, his military leadership hinted at; but not a word is said of the land and its conquest and settlement. A silence (not noted by Clines) as deafening as that of the Balaam narratives. We may certainly agree with Noth[31] that a description of the *settlement* lay outside P's interests. Our question must be just how far 'the land' even as an unfulfilled goal may be deemed a *dominant* feature in Num. 1–27. It is much clearer that Deuteronomy and Joshua reach back to the past than that (the first three-quarters of) Numbers looks forwards.[32]

(4) *Some wider issues*

In our Preface we quoted Wellhausen's opinion that Joshua is an appendix to the Pentateuch, assuming it at all points. Our study has shown rather that the end of Numbers is something of an appendix, which assumes the book of Joshua at all points. We feel we have more than vindicated Noth's assertion of the significance of the study of Joshua for the understanding of the Pentateuch. Yet just how much of the Pentateuch stands to gain illumination from our conclusions? We may have plotted the development of the biblical theme of Israel's distribution of the land of Canaan. We may have clarified some of the issues posed as 'Tetrateuch-Pentateuch-Hexateuch' by Mowinckel. Yet in doing so we have stressed the distinctiveness of Deuteronomy within the Pentateuch and emphasized the lateness of the chapters at the end of Numbers. And so, even granted the validity of our arguments, just what may they have contributed to study of the *Pentateuch*—rather than only a readily isolable part of it?

Before sketching an answer to this question we should remind ourselves how far our arguments were made possible by the plentiful availability of contrasting source-material. The existence of very similar yet strikingly different information in Jos. 21 and 1 Chron. 6, in Jud. 1 and scattered parts of Joshua, and in the second half of Joshua and the end of Numbers, demanded explanation. And each set of problems was illuminated by the study of another pair of parallel texts—our inherited Hebrew and Greek versions of Joshua. The situation is very different in the rest of the Pentateuch: there are few extra-Pentateuchal parallels to its narrative or its legislation, and there is much less variety in the testimony to its text than is the case in Joshua. How far are our findings applicable to the rest of the Pentateuch?

We have documented the creative re-handling of tradition within the emergent biblical material of early Judaism, long after its commitment to writing, and even (with some probability) after the division of this material into the 'books' with which we are familiar. Literary and textual criticism are intimately and necessarily related today, because the divergences in our inherited textual traditions result from a continuation of the very processes of composition that produced the parent text from which both diverged. Written tradition had been far from fixed, yet it was not uncontrolled. Many of the adjustments made later to the books studied were effected on the authority of other elements within the developing 'scriptural' corpus. Some of these, bringing what Jos. 5 reports about circumcision and passover into line with developed 'Priestly' tradition, signal the authority of the Pentateuch. Yet it would be surprising if it had only been at the end of Numbers that contributions were received into that Pentateuch.

We have noted that these late chapters in Numbers owe much of their content and terminology to material familiar to us in Deuteronomy, Joshua, and Ezekiel. But their literary framework is like so much of Leviticus and Numbers. How much more of the legislation in these books was added around the same time? It would be surprising if it were only the details of Joshua's work that had later been found to require the stamp of Moses' authority.

We have shown time and time again how the removal of a few supplementary verses and phrases can open new vistas for the appreciation of the 'host' text; and have shown too, as just noted above, that it was standard 'Priestly' formulae that were used to append the instructions on the land to the book of Numbers. These observations can only strengthen the hands of those who treat the P texts in Genesis at least as supplements to an inherited text, not the beginning of a base-narrative into which all the rest was fitted.

Two comments may be appropriate here: One is to recall Fohrer's comments about P[33] to which he ascribed Num. 28–31, 33–36. He recognized the problem of literary unity in the P-material, yet regarded it in its totality as an independent intellectual unit. The case for literary disunity seems clear. What is problematic is the claim of intellectual independence. There is distinctive terminology; there is the repeated claim that what is to be preserved, what is to be asserted, is what was revealed through Moses at Sinai or at least before his death. Yet the production of these closing chapters of Numbers was slavishly *dependent* on the development within a somewhat different environment of the second half of Joshua.

The other concerns Clines' claim that his method of studying the Pentateuch involves a move from the *known* to the (relatively) unknown.[34] We too have sought to make the known our starting point, but have moved from it in a rather different direction. We think we have assembled enough evidence to *prove* (bold word) that the end of Numbers and the whole of Deuteronomy were late additions to the Pentateuch. Our discussion of the biblical sources (actual, not hypothetical!) has attested the use of techniques of composition in the familiar Pentateuch and Joshua similar to those in chapters 18 and 20 of the Samaritan Exodus.[35] The removal of these later additions may allow quite as much (and possibly even more) sense to be made of the remainder of the corpus as Clines makes of the present Pentateuch.

Most criticism of the Pentateuch has started at its beginning, with the detection of parallel accounts from creation onwards. We have sought to demonstrate that a more fruitful start from the known Pentateuch can be made at its end—in two senses of that word: by unravelling first the knots tied *last*, and by recognizing the extensive appendices at the Pentateuch's *conclusion*. Does that mean that the sole contribution of this study to criticism of the Pentateuch as a whole has been the plotting of some obstacles whose removal will permit a clearer view of the rest?

Perhaps. But another possibility deserves to be stated. Mention of one further recent study may suffice to make our question more insistent. Nicholson seems to have presented the case convincingly that it was from Deuteronomy that the Decalogue was introduced to the Sinai story of Exodus.[36] It was only after the Decalogue achieved prominence within Deuteronomy, as the 'text' of which all that followed in the book was the exposition, that it was inserted in a similarly prominent position in Exodus —so displacing the 'Book of the Covenant' as the core of the legislation at Sinai.[37] Such a theory explains the Deuteronomic affinities of the Exodus 20 version as well as its 'Priestly' links over sabbath and creation. How exceptional is this further example of 'Priestly' appropriation of material developed in another biblical context? Like the appendices on which this study has concentrated, it has an identifiable source; unlike them, it was not placed at the end of the corpus. Unlike perhaps any other major addition to the body of the Pentateuch, its source is available for inspection and discussion.[38] But is its very presence justification for a search for other such supplements, even if their immediate source is beyond our ken? Have we succeeded in broadening the empirical basis of Pentateuchal analysis?

NOTES

1. 'Von der Liste zur Beschreibung', pp. 5–8.
2. The descriptions of the territories of the 'six' employ *'br*/'cross' only twice in 29 verbal forms; in the other texts it appears 12 times out of 45. (The comparable statistics for the other common verb, *yṣ'*/'proceed' are eight and thirteen.)
3. Noth's attempts to link the description of Dan and the town-lists of Benjamin with the town-lists of Judah were recalled above, p. 37. We have not attempted to decide whether, as in the case of Judah and Benjamin, both town-lists and border-descriptions appeared in this first draft of Joshua, or which may have been prior. That must be the business of another study.
4. The elaboration of these notes is discussed in detail in my article in *VT* 25, especially pp. 279–282 which treats the most complex of them (Jos. 17:11–13). In that discussion I noted that *bnwt(yh)*, '(its) dependent villages' is used only in apparently late texts, and much more often in Nehemiah and Chronicles than elsewhere in the Bible.
5. In MT, at 1 Kings 9:16, 17. However in LXX the information appears after 1 Kings 5:14, and also at the end of Jos. 16:10.
6. *VT* 25, p. 285. Kallai (*IEJ* 28, 1978, 254–255) reflects a similar approach when he notes that Jud. 1 is a 'compound chapter' which 'is based on the general concept of the book of Joshua'.
7. My argument, *op. cit.*, that Jud. 1 was drafted as a new introduction when the familiar division into 'books' of Joshua, Judges, etc. was made appears to have been accepted by Smend (*Entstehung*, p. 115).
8. *VT* 25, p. 278.
9. Cf. above, pp. 60–61.
10. Joshua had been rounded off as a 'book' at the same time as Judges.
11. Cf. above, p. 42.
12. This issue may have been clarified in Mittmann's *Beiträge* with which regrettably I am still not familiar.
13. Jos. 21:10b–12 and 1 Chron. 6:39b–41.
14. Cf. *ZAW* 91, p. 197.
15. His notes in 21:4, 10 that the Aaronites were of the Kohathite family, and a (priestly) section of the Levites are additional to the source-material from Chronicles which calls them simply *bny 'hrn*.
16. On p. 79 above, I noted that v. 6 was a supplement to the first draft of Num. 35:1–8. It may be that even what remains has undergone development—the total of 48 cities (v. 7) may be held to imply a uniform grant of four cities from each of twelve tribes, while the following verse specifies an uneven grant proportional to tribal size.
17. On p. 80 above we found it impossible to decide which was the prior text.
18. It had probably become a book between stages two and three.
19. Another of the links between Joshua and Chronicles discussed by Japhet (*JBL* 98, 208–213)—cf. also p. 101, n. 17 above—could be alternatively presented, with implications for the dating of Smend's DtrN. She notes that Shihor of Egypt and Lebo Hammath are paired only in Jos. 13:1–7 and 1 Chron. 13:5—but not Smend's point that the description of the land that remains is a (corrective) supplement to the core of Jos. 13:1–7. If that view is acceptable, it may be appropriate to move in a different direction from her observation that the view of Israel's settlement in 1 Chron. 13:5, while unprecedented, is also part and parcel of the Chronicler's general view of the

historical process; that 'whereas certain isolated elements of the Chronicler's view are taken from earlier biblical sources, the concept as a whole is unique and does not conform to any of the preceding historical accounts' (p. 212). What I am suggesting is that it may be as true of Jos. 13:2–6 as of 17:11–13 that the earlier draft of Joshua has been accommodated to material in Chronicles. If it is true that Num. 34:2 depends on Jos. 13:6, the implications for dating that early stratum of the end of Numbers would have to be drawn accordingly. Another possible solution to this dilemma might be that Jos. 13:2–6 and 17:11–13 are composite. I have already suggested this for the latter passage in *VT* 25, 280–281. May it be that 13:3–5 ('from Shihor of Egypt . . . to Lebo Hammath') is a supplement to 13:2, 6; and that in *both* Joshua passages it is DtrN that has been supplemented from Chronicles?

20. A broader discussion is offered in an article in the *Expository Times* 91 (1980), 'Keeping up with Recent Studies: VI. The Pentateuch'.
21. Rendtorff's questions were prefigured in 'Der "Jahwist" als Theologe?', read at the Edinburgh Congress in 1974, and developed in *Das Überlieferungsgeschichtliche Problem des Pentateuch*, 1977. For the sake of brevity, only his new approach is discussed here although elements of it are shared by Schmid's *Der sogenannte Jahwist*, 1976, and Van Seters' *Abraham in History and Tradition*, 1975.
22. The whole number of *JSOT* 3, 1977, was devoted to the discussion; and McKane has offered a substantial and appreciative review of Rendtorff's *Problem* in *VT* 28, 1978.
23. *Problem*, p. 27.
24. *op. cit.*, pp. 158ff., esp. pp. 166–167.
25. And this for two reasons: (a) because this later material in Joshua was not obviously influenced by Deuteronomy; (b) because, if we are right that the book division had taken place, Joshua was no longer part of a Deuteronomistic History.
26. *Hexateucherzählung*, pp. 11–12.
27. Brekelmans, 'Die sogenannten deuteronomischen Elemente', 1966.
28. Some elements of this study were noted above, pp. 92–93. These and others I have discussed in my review of the book in *JSOT* 8, 1978.
29. As suggested in our discussion of Tengström in chapter VI above, it is surprising that he does not mention the possibility that these passages could be Deuteronomic and expanded by *later* Deuteronomic material—even to refute it.
30. This brief discussion of Clines, *The Theme of the Pentateuch*, 1978, concentrates on pp. 29, 53–57, 89–96.
31. Cf. above, p. 7.
32. Deuteronomy (and Joshua) frequently mention the promises to the fathers, the freedom from Egypt, the law-giving at the mountain; and Deuteronomy opens with the narrative of the passage through Transjordan. It is a pity that Rendtorff nowhere mentions Deut. 1–3 in connection with his suggestion that parallel texts in Numbers 'bear a Deuteronomic stamp'. Why should Deuteronomic circles have helped collect material in Numbers, then redrafted it afresh in Deuteronomy?
33. Cf. above, p. 47.
34. Clines, *Theme*, p. 89.
35. Tigay has adduced this Smaritan material in his proposal of an 'Empirical Basis for the Documentary Hypothesis'. But it appears more closely analogous to the methods we have been discussing than to those of what is normally termed the Documentary Hypothesis.
36. Nicholson, 'The Decalogue as the direct address of God', *VT* 27, 1977.
37. This would then be a precursor of the additions to the text of Exodus from

Deuteronomy noted by Tigay.

38. Such relocation of the Decalogue is a matter not of harmonization, but rather of creative restructuring of tradition. It is important to recognize that key structural elements of the present text need not have been part of all earlier drafts. Even if we grant that the use of the verb *kbš* in connection with the noun *'rṣ* in both Gen. 1:28 and some texts in Joshua is not coincidental, that is far from adequate ground for ascribing both to the basic stratum of P (cf. Lohfink's argument described above on p. 70, n. 57 and p. 87, n. 52). These supplements to Joshua may have been drafted with Gen. 1:28 in mind; or Gen. 1:28 may have been supplemented with these texts from Joshua in mind. Either seems in principle possible, and a decision would require quite tight criteria.

BIBLIOGRAPHY*

Abel, F. M. *Le Livre de Josué*, Bible de Jérusalem, Paris, ²1958.
Aharoni, Y. 'The Negeb of Judah', *IEJ* 8, 1958, 26–38.
—— 'The Province List of Judah', *VT* 9, 1959, 225–246.
—— *The Land of the Bible*, London, 1967.
—— 'Rubute and Ginti-Kirmil', *VT* 19, 1969, 137–145.
Alt, A. 'Judas Gaue unter Josia', 1925: in *KS* II, München, 1953, 276–288.
—— 'Das System der Stämmesgrenzen im Buche Josua', 1927: in *KS* I, München, 1953, 193–202.
—— 'Eine galiläische Ortsliste in Jos. 19', *ZAW* 45, 1927, 59–81.
Anderson, G. W. *A Critical Introduction to the Old Testament*, London, 1959.
Astruc, J. *Conjectures sur les mémoires originaux dont il paroit que Moyse s'est servi pour composer le livre de la Genèse. Avec des Remarques, que appuient ou qui éclaircissent ces Conjectures*, Bruxelles, 1753.
Auld, A. G. 'Judges 1 and History: a Reconstruction', *VT* 25, 1975, 261–285.
—— *Studies in Joshua: Text and Literary Relations*, unpubl. Ph.D. Thesis, University of Edinburgh, 1976.
—— 'A Judean Sanctuary of 'Anat (Josh. 15:59)?', *Tel Aviv* 4, 1977, 85–86.
—— review of S. Tengström, *Die Hexateucherzählung*: in *JSOT* 8, 1978, 71–74.
—— 'Cities of Refuge in Israelite Tradition', *JSOT* 10, 1978, 26–40.
—— 'Textual and Literary Studies in the Book of Joshua', *ZAW* 90, 1978, 412–417.
—— 'The "Levitical Cities": Texts and History', *ZAW* 91, 1979, 194–206.
—— 'Joshua: the Hebrew and Greek Texts', *Studies in the Historical Books of the OT*, VT Suppl. 30, 1979, 1–14.

* The following is the list of the works cited, often more briefly, in the course of the work. It makes no attempt to offer a full bibliography of the several topics discussed.

—— 'Keeping up with Recent Studies. VI. The Pentateuch', *ExT*, 91, 1980, 297–302.

Bächli, O. 'Von der Liste zur Beschreibung' *ZDPV* 89, 1973, 1–14.

Beltz, W. *Die Kaleb-Traditionen im Alten Testament*, BWANT 98, Stuttgart, 1974.

Blenkinsopp, J. 'The Structure of P', *CBQ* 38, 1976, 275–292.

Brekelmans, C. 'Die sogenannte deuteronomistische Elemente in Genesis bis Numeri', *Geneva Congress Volume*, VT Suppl. 15, 1966, 90–96.

Bright, J. 'Joshua: Introduction and Exegesis', *Interpreter's Bible* 2, New York—Nashville, 1953, 539–693.

Brueggemann, W. 'The Kerygma of the Priestly Writers', *ZAW* 84, 1972, 397–414.

Clements, R. E. *Prophecy and Tradition*, Oxford, 1975.

Clines, D. J. A. *The Theme of the Pentateuch*, JSOT Suppl. Ser. 10, Sheffield, 1978.

Cross, F. M. *Canaanite Myth and Hebrew Epic*, Cambridge (Mass.), 1973.

Cross, F. M. & Wright, G. E. 'The Boundary and Province Lists of the Kingdom of Judah', *JBL* 75, 1956, 202–226.

Dietrich, W. *Prophetie und Geschichte*, FRLANT 108, Göttingen, 1972.

Dus, J. 'Die Analyse zweier Ladeerzählungen des Josuabuches (Jos. 3–4 und 6)', *ZAW* 72, 1960, 107–134.

Ehrlich, A. B. *Randglossen zur hebräischen Bibel* III, Leipzig, 1910.

Eissfeldt, O. *Hexateuch-Synopse*, Leipzig, 1922 (=Darmstadt, ^{2}1962).

—— 'Die Geschichtswerke im Alten Testament', *ThLZ* 72, 1947, cc. 71–76.

—— *Die Geschichtsschreibung im Alten Testament*, Berlin, 1948.

—— *The Old Testament: An Introduction*, Oxford, 1965.

—— 'Deuteronomium und Hexateuch', 1966: in *KS* IV, Tübingen, 1968, 238–258.

Engnell, I. *Gamla Testamentet. En Traditionshistorisk Inledning* I, Stockholm, 1945.

—— 'Prophets and Prophetism in the Old Testament', *Critical Essays on the Old Testament*, London, 1970, 123–179.

Fohrer, G. *Introduction to the Old Testament*, London, 1970.

Fritz, V. *Israel in der Wüste*, Marburg, 1970.

Fuss, W. *Die deuteronomistische Pentateuchredaktion in Ex. 3–17*, BZAW 126, 1972.

Gerleman, G. 'Nutzrecht und Wohnrecht', *ZAW* 89, 1977, 313–325.

Gray, J. *Joshua, Judges and Ruth*, New Century Bible, London, 1967.

Hertzberg, H. W. *Die Bücher Josua, Richter, Ruth*, ATD 9, Göttingen, ^{3}1965.

Holmes, S. *Joshua, the Hebrew and Greek Texts*, Cambridge, 1914.

Hölscher, G. *Die Anfänge der hebräischen Geschichtsschreibung*, Heidelberg, 1942.

—— *Geschichtsschreibung in Israel*, Lund, 1952.
Japhet, S. 'Conquest and Settlement in Chronicles', *JBL* 98, 1979, 205–218.
Jenni, E. 'Zwei Jahrzehnte Forschung an den Büchern Josua bis Könige', *ThR* 27, 1961/2, 1–32, 97–146.
Kallai, Z. 'The Town lists of Judah, Simeon, Benjamin and Dan', *VT* 8, 1958, 134–160.
—— *nḥlwt šbṭy yśr'l*, Jerusalem, 1967.
—— 'The United Monarchy of Israel—A Focal Point in Israelite Historiography', *IEJ* 27, 1977, 103–109.
—— 'Organizational and Administrative Frameworks in the Kingdom of David and Solomon', *Proceedings of the Sixth World Congress in Jewish Studies*, I, Jerusalem, 1977, 213–220.
—— 'Judah and Israel—A Study in Israelite Historiography', *IEJ* 28, 1978, 251–261.
Kaufmann, Y. *The Biblical Account of the Conquest of Palestine*, Jerusalem, 1953.
—— *spr yhwš'*, Jerusalem, 1959.
Kraus, H.-J. 'Gilgal. Ein Beitrag zur Kultgeschichte Israels', *VT* 1, 1951, 181–199.
Langlamet, F. *Gilgal et les Récits de la Traversée du Jourdain*, Cahiers de la Révue Biblique 11, Paris, 1969.
—— 'Josue, II, et les Traditions de l'Hexateuque', *RB* 78, 1971, 5–17, 161–183, 321–354.
—— 'La Traversée du Jordain et les Documents de l'Hexateuque', *RB* 79, 1972, 7–38.
Lohfink, N. 'Die Priesterschrift und die Geschichte', *Göttingen Congress Volume*, VT Suppl. 29, 1978, 189–225.
McKane, W. review of R. Rendtorff, *Das überl. Problem:* in *VT* 28, 1978, 371–382.
Maier, J. *Das Altisraelitische Ladeheiligtum*, BZAW 93, 1965.
Margolis, M. A. *The Book of Joshua in Greek*, Paris, 1931/8.
May, H. G. 'Joshua', *Peake's Commentary on the Bible*, London, 1962, 289–303.
Mazar, B. 'The Cities of the Priests and the Levites', *VT Suppl.* 7, 1960, 193–205.
—— 'The Cities of the Territory of Dan', *IEJ* 10, 1960, 65–77.
Miller, J. M. & Tucker, G. M. *The Book of Joshua*, Cambridge Bible Commentary, Cambridge, 1974.
Mittmann, S. *Beiträge zur Siedlungs- und Territorialgeschichte des nördlichen Ostjordanlandes*, Wiesbaden, 1970.
—— *Deuteronomium 1:1–6:3 literarkritisch und traditions-geschichtlich untersucht*, BZAW 139, 1975.
Möhlenbrink, K. 'Die Landnahmesagen des Buches Josua', *ZAW* 56,

1938, 238–268.
Mowinckel, S. 'Julius Wellhausen', *Norsk Kirkeblad* 15, 1918, 306–312.
—— 'Julius Wellhausen', *For Kirke og Kultur*, 25, 1918, 277–288.
—— review of O. Eissfeldt, *Hexateuch-Synopse*: in *Norsk Teologisk Tidsskrift*, 1923, 195–202.
—— 'L'Origine du Décalogue', *Révue d'Histoire et de Philosophie Réligieuses* (Strasbourg) 6, 1926, 409–433, 501–525.
—— *Le Décalogue*, Paris, 1927.
—— 'Der Ursprung der Bileamsage', *ZAW* 48, 1930, 233–271.
—— 'Hat es ein israelitisches Nationalepos gegeben?', *ZAW* 53, 1935, 130–152.
—— *The Two Sources of the Pre-Deuteronomic Primeval History (JE) in Gen. 1–11*, Oslo, 1937.
—— *Prophecy and Tradition*, Oslo, 1946.
—— *Zur Frage nach dokumentarischen Quellen in Joshua 13–19*, Oslo, 1946.
—— 'Die vermeintliche "Passahlegende" Ex. 1–15', *StTh* 5, 1951, 66–88.
—— 'Israelite Historiography', *ASTI* 2, 1963, 4–26.
—— *Erwägungen zur Pentateuch Quellenfrage*, Oslo, 1964 (cited: *Erwägungen*).
—— *Tetrateuch-Pentateuch-Hexateuch. Die Berichte über die Landnahme in den drei altisraelitischen Geschichtswerken*, BZAW 90, 1964 (cited: T-P-H).
—— *Kanaan for Israel*, Oslo, 1967.
—— *Israels opphav og eldste historie*, Oslo, 1967.
——, Michelet, S. & Messel, N. *Det Gamle Testamente* I (Loven), Oslo, 1929.
Nicholson, E. W. *Exodus and Sinai in History and Tradition*, Oxford, 1973.
—— 'The Decalogue as the direct address of God', *VT* 27, 1977, 422–433.
Noth, M. *Das System der zwölf Stämme Israels*, BWANT 4.1, Stuttgart, 1930.
—— 'Studien zu den historisch-geographischen Dokumenten des Josuabuches', *ZDPV* 58, 1935, 185–255.
—— *Das Buch Josua*, HAT I, 7, Tübingen, 1938, ²1953 (cited: *Josua*).
—— 'Numeri 21 als Glied der "Hexateuch"-Erzählung', *ZAW* 58, 1940/1, 161–189.
—— *Überlieferungsgeschichtliche Studien* I, Halle, 1943 (cited: *UGS*).
—— *Überlieferungsgeschichte des Pentateuch*, 1948: Eng. Trans., *A History of Pentateuchal Traditions*, Englewood Cliffs, N.J., 1972 (cited: HPT).
—— 'Überlieferungsgeschichtliches zur zweiten Hälfte des Josuabuches', *Bonner Biblische Beiträge* 1, 1950, 152–167.
—— *The History of Israel*, London, ²1960.
—— *Exodus*, OTL, London, 1962.

—— *Leviticus*, OTL, London, 1965.
—— *Numbers*, OTL, London, 1968.
Nyberg, H. S. *Studien zum Hoseabuche*, Uppsala, 1935.
Oded, B. summary of Z. Kallai, *nḥlwt šbṭy yśr'l*: in *Immanuel* 1, 1972, 19–20.
Orlinsky, H. M. 'The Hebrew *Vorlage* of the Septuagint of the Book of Joshua', *Rome Congress Volume*, VT Suppl. 17, 1969, 187–195.
Otto, E. *Das Mazzotfest in Gilgal*, BWANT 107, Stuttgart, 1975.
Pedersen, J. 'Passahfest und Passahlegende', *ZAW* 52, 1934, 161–175.
—— *Israel* III–IV, London, 1940.
Porter, J. R. 'The Succession of Joshua': in Durham, J. I. and Porter, J. R. (ed.), *Proclamation and Presence*, London, 1970.
—— 'The Background of Joshua III–V', *Svensk Exegetisk Årsbok* 36, 1971, 5–23.
von Rad, G. *Die Priesterschrift im Hexateuch*, Stuttgart, 1934.
—— 'The Form-Critical Problem of the Hexateuch', 1938: in *The Problem of the Hexateuch and Other Essays*, Edinburgh, 1966, 1–78.
—— 'Hexateuch oder Pentateuch?', *VuF* 1947/8, 1949/50, 52–56.
—— 'Literarkritische und überlieferungsgeschichtliche Forschung im Alten Testament', *VuF* 1947/8, 1949/50, 172–194.
—— *Old Testament Theology* I/II, Edinburgh, 1962/5.
Redford, D. B. *A Study of the Biblical Story of Joseph* (*Genesis 37–50*), VT Suppl. 20, 1970.
Rendtorff, R. 'The "Yahwist" as Theologian? The Dilemma of Pentateuchal Criticism', 1975: in *JSOT* 3, 1977, 2–10.
—— *Das überlieferungsgeschichtliche Problem des Pentateuch*, BZAW 147, 1977.
Rofé, A. 'The End of the Book of Joshua according to the Septuagint', *Shnaton* 1, 1977, 217–227 (Hebrew, with English summary).
Rost, L. *Das kleine Credo und andere Studien zum Alten Testament*, Heidelberg, 1965.
Rudolph, W. *Der 'Elohist' von Exodus bis Josua*, BZAW 68, 1938.
Schmid, H. H. *Der sogenannte Jahwist: Beobachtungen und Fragen zur Pentateuchforschung*, Zürich, 1976.
Schmid, R. 'Meerwunder- und Landnahmetraditionen', *ThZ* 21, 1965, 260–268.
Schunck, K.-D. *Benjamin*, BZAW 86, 1963.
Seidel, H. 'Der Untergang Jerichos (Jos. 6)—Exegese ohne Kerygma?', *Theologische Versuche* VIII, 1977.
Simons, J. *The Geographical and Topographical Texts of the Old Testament*, Leiden, 1959.
Simpson, C. A. *The Early Traditions of Israel. A Critical Analysis of the Pre-Deuteronomic Narrative of the Hexateuch*, Oxford, 1948.
Smend, R. (sen.) *Die Erzählung des Hexateuch auf ihren Quellen untersucht*,

Berlin, 1912.
Smend, R. (jun.) 'Das Gesetz und die Völker', in Wolff, H. W. (ed.), *Probleme Biblischer Theologie*, München, 1971, 494–509.
—— *Die Entstehung des Alten Testaments*, Stuttgart, 1978.
Soggin, J. A. 'Gilgal, Passah und Landnahme', *Geneva Congress Volume*, VT Suppl. 15, 1966, 263–277.
—— *Joshua*, OTL, London, 1972.
—— *Introduction to the Old Testament: From its Origins to the Closing of the Alexandrian Canon*, OTL, London, 1976.
Stähelin, J. J. 'Beiträge zu den kritischen Untersuchungen über den Pentateuch, die Bücher Josua und der Richter', *Theologische Studien und Kritiken* 8, 1835, 461ff.
Strange, J. 'The Inheritance of Dan', *StTh* 20, 1966, 120–139.
Sturdy, J. *Numbers*, Cambridge Bible Commentary, Cambridge, 1976.
Tengström, S. *Die Hexateucherzählung: eine literaturgeschichtliche Studie*, Coniectanea Biblica, OT Ser. 7, Lund, 1976.
Tigay, J. H. 'An Empirical Basis for the Documentary Hypothesis', *JBL* 94, 1975, 329–342.
Van Seters, J. *Abraham in History and Tradition*, London, 1975.
de Vaux, R. 'Reflections on the Present State of Pentateuchal Criticism', 1953: in *The Bible and the Ancient Near East*, London, 1972, 31–48.
—— *The Early History of Israel*, London, 1978.
Vink, J. G. 'The Date and Origin of the Priestly Code', *OTS* 15, 1969, 1–144.
Vogt, E. 'Die Erzählung vom Jordanübergang Josua 3–4', *Biblica* 66, 1965, 125–148.
Vriezen, T. C. 'Exodusstudien: Exodus I', *VT* 17, 1967, 334–353.
Weimar, P. *Untersuchungen zur Redaktionsgeschichte des Pentateuch*, BZAW 146, 1977.
Weinfeld, M. *Deuteronomy and the Deuteronomic School*, Oxford, 1972.
Weiser, A. *Introduction to the Old Testament*, London, 1961.
Wellhausen, J. *Die Composition des Hexateuchs*, Berlin, ^{3}1899.
—— *Prolegomena to the History of Israel*, Edinburgh, 1885.
de Wette, W. M. L. *Beiträge zur Einleitung in das Alte Testament*, Halle, 1806/7.
Wijngaards, J. N. M. *The Dramatization of Salvific History in the Deuteronomic Schools*, OTS 16, 1969.
Wilcoxen, J. A. 'Narrative Structure and Cult Legend: a Study of Joshua 1–6', in Rylaarsdam, J. C. (ed.), *Transitions in Biblical Scholarship*, Chicago and London, 1968, 43–70.
Wüst, M. *Untersuchungen zu den siedlungsgeographischen Texten des Alten Testaments: I. Ostjordanland*, Wiesbaden, 1975.

INDEX OF SELECT HEBREW WORDS AND PHRASES

INDEX OF AUTHORS

INDEX OF BIBLICAL NAMES

(For some further references, consult also the Hebrew Index.)

SUBJECT AND GENERAL INDEX

INDEX OF BIBLICAL REFERENCES